LACAN: IN SPITE OF EVERYTHING

LACAN: IN SPITE OF EVERYTHING

ÉLISABETH ROUDINESCO

Translated by
Gregory Elliott

VERSO
London • New York

Liberté • Égalité • Fraternité
RÉPUBLIQUE FRANÇAISE

This book is supported by the Institut français as part of the Burgess Programme (www.frenchbooknews.com)

This English-language edition first published by Verso 2014
Translation © Gregory Elliott 2014
Previously published as *Lacan, envers et contre tout*
© Seuil 2011

1 3 5 7 9 10 8 6 4 2

Verso
UK: 6 Meard Street, London W1F 0EG
US: 20 Jay Street, Suite 1010, Brooklyn, NY 11201
www.versobooks.com

Verso is the imprint of New Left Books

ISBN-13: 978-1-78168-162-6 (PBK)
ISBN-13: 978-1-78168-163-3 (HBK)
eISBN-13: 978-1-78168-214-2 (US)
eISBN-13: 978-1-78168-640-9 (UK)

British Library Cataloguing in Publication Data
A catalogue record for this book is available from the British Library.

Library of Congress Cataloging-in-Publication Data
A catalog record for this book is available from the Library of Congress.

Typeset in Sabon by Hewer Text UK Ltd, Edinburgh, Scotland
Printed in the US by Maple Press

Watch my *Télévision*. I'm a clown. Let it be an example to you and don't imitate me!

Jacques Lacan

Since he has to teach . . . doctors, analysts or analysands, in the rhetoric of his speech Lacan provides them with a dumbshow equivalent of the language of the unconscious which, as is well known, is in its ultimate essence '*Witz*', successful or unsuccessful pun and metaphor.

Louis Althusser

CONTENTS

1

THIRTY YEARS AFTER

Since the publication in 1993 of part three of my *History of Psychoanalysis*, wholly devoted to the thought, life, oeuvre and career of Jacques Lacan,[1] I have often felt I would one day need to draw up a balance sheet not only of the legacy of this paradoxical master, but also of the way my own work was received within the psychoanalytical community and outside it.

No doubt I had mistakenly imagined that an objective work, based on a critical approach, would be such as to calm passions. And that perhaps Marc Bloch's famous sentence – 'Robespierrists! Anti-Robespierrists!

1. In English see Élisabeth Roudinesco, *Jacques Lacan: An Outline of a Life and History of a System of Thought*, trans. Barbara Bray, New York, Columbia University Press, 1997, and *Jacques Lacan & Co.: A History of Psychoanalysis in France, 1925–1985*, trans. Jeffrey Mehlman, London, Free Association, 1990. A new, revised and corrected French edition of the original volumes was published as *Histoire de la psychanalyse en France – Jacques Lacan*, Paris, Le Livre de Poche, 2009.

For pity's sake, simply tell us what Robespierre was!'[2]
– which I used as an epigraph to my book, would finally
make it possible to consider the fate of the man and the
development of his thought dispassionately. While the
result was largely positive, it is clear that the man and
his work continue to be subject to the most extravagant
interpretations, at a time when every generation has a
tendency to forget what occurred prior to it – unless,
that is, it is engaged in celebration of the patrimonial,
genealogical precedence of a supposed 'golden age',
rather than in a reflection on the past that can throw
light on the future.

Compounding this are the deliria that periodically
emerge from unscrupulous polemicists or therapists
who crave notoriety: Lacan as a Nazi, anti-Semitic,
incestuous, criminal, fraudulent Freud; Lacan as a
pervert, wild beast, Maoist, rapist, leader of a sect,
charlatan, who beat his wives, patients, domestics and
children, and collected firearms. Everything has been
said on this subject and the rumour mill is in
overdrive.

Our age is individualistic and pragmatic. It loves the
present moment, estimation, economic determinism,
opinion polls, immediacy, relativism and security. It culti-
vates rejection of commitment and elites, contempt for
thinking, transparency, enjoyment of evil and perverse
sex, and the expression of feelings and emotions against a

---

2. Marc Bloch, *The Historian's Craft*, trans. Peter Putnam,
Manchester, Manchester University Press, 1992, p. 116.

background of explaining human beings by their neurons or genes – as if a mono-causality could account for the human condition. The rise of populism in Europe, and the attraction it holds for some intellectuals who openly advocate racism, xenophobia and nationalism, are probably not unconnected to this state of affairs.

It must be said that the advent of a wild capitalism has contributed to the planetary extension of despair and misery, associated with the reactivation of religious fanaticism which serves as a political reference-point and sense of identity for some. In France, eight million people suffer from mental health problems and treat themselves as best they can: drugs, various kinds of therapy, alternative medicines, cures of every kind, personal development, healing, and so forth. Throughout the democratic world, self-doctoring practices are expanding immeasurably, to the exclusion of science and, invariably, reason. In this world the quest for pleasure – not collective happiness – has replaced the aspiration to truth. And because psychoanalysis is committed to the search for self-truth, it has come into contradiction with the dual tendency towards hedonism, on the one hand, and a retreat into identity, on the other.

By the same token, however, our age generates challenges to what it presents: it is when danger is at its height, said Hölderlin, that deliverance is at hand[3] – as is hope. The proof? After three decades of ridiculous critiques of the very idea of rebellion, we witness the

---

3. 'But where danger is/Deliverance also grows' (Hölderlin, *Patmos*).

emergence of a new desire for Revolution, outside Europe where it was born.

As regards the history and historiography of psychoanalysis, it is as if, despite the rigorous establishment of the facts and the exploration of several multi-faceted truths, Lacan – in the wake of Freud and all his heirs – were still regarded sometimes as a devil, sometimes as an idol. Hence Manichaeism and a denegation of history. And psychoanalysts are not to be outdone: jargon, melancholic posture, closure to social questions, nostalgia. They prefer memory to history, reiteration to establishing the facts, love of the old days to that of the present. They readily forget that 'tomorrow is another day' – to the extent that we are entitled to ask whether they do not sometimes conduct themselves as enemies of their discipline and inheritance.

It was in registering this state of affairs, and while observing the signs of a new hope, that I wanted – thirty years after Lacan's death, at a time when the gradual passing of a certain (supposedly 'heroic') age of psychoanalysis is evident and psychoanalysts are turning into organized psychotherapists in a profession regulated by the state – to speak differently, and more personally this time. To speak of the fate of the last great thinker in an intellectual adventure that began to have an impact at the end of the nineteenth century, during the slow decline of the Austro-Hungarian Empire and the institutions bound up with it: the patriarchal family, monarchical sovereignty, the cult of tradition, a refusal of the future.

Addressing today's readers, I wanted to evoke some striking episodes in a life and oeuvre with which a whole generation was involved, and comment on them with the benefit of hindsight, freely and subjectively. I would like this book to be read as the exposition of a secret part of the life and work of Lacan, a wandering off the beaten track: a reverse or dark side emerging to illuminate the record, as in an encrypted painting where the shadowy figures, formerly hidden, return to the light. Bit by bit, I wanted to evoke a *different* Lacan confronted with his excesses, his 'passion for the real',[4] his objects – in a word, his real, what has been foreclosed from his symbolic universe. A Lacan of the margins, the edges, the literal, carried away by his mania for neologisms.

This Lacan heralded the times that have become ours, foresaw the rise of racism and communitarianism, the passion for ignorance and hatred of thinking, the loss of the privileges of masculinity and the excesses of a wild femininity, the advent of a depressive society, the impasses of Enlightenment and Revolution, the struggle to the death between science elevated to a religion, religion elevated to a discourse of science, and man reduced to his biological being: 'Before long', he said in 1971, 'we are going to be submerged by problems of segregation which will be called racism and which stem from control of what occurs at the level of the reproduction

---

4. Alain Badiou, *The Century*, trans. Alberto Toscano, Cambridge, Polity Press, 2007, p. 48.

of life among beings who, by virtue of the fact that they speak, discover that they have all sorts of problems of consciousness . . .'[5]

To discuss Lacan again, thirty years after his death, is also to recall an intellectual adventure that holds an important place in our modernity, and whose legacy remains fertile whatever people may say: freedom of speech and mores; the development of numerous forms of emancipation – of women, minorities, homosexuals; the hope of changing life, the family, madness, schools and desire; and a rejection of norms and the pleasure of transgression.

Arousing the jealousy of experts who have never stopped abusing him, Lacan positioned himself against the current of these hopes, like some lucid, disenchanted libertine. Certainly, he was convinced that the search for truth was the only way to replace salvation by progress, obscurantism by enlightenment. But only on condition, he said, that we realize that rationality can always turn into its opposite and bring about its own destruction. Hence his defence of rites, traditions and symbolic structures. Those who reject him today, making him into what he never was and saddling him with the defamatory label of 'guru' or 'scourge of democracy', forget that, sometimes against himself, he immersed himself deeply in these changes – to the extent of embracing their paradoxes through his language

---

5. Jacques Lacan, *Le Séminaire. Livre XIX, . . . ou pire* (1971–72), Paris, Seuil, 2011.

games and wordplay, which we enjoy practising today. The twentieth century was Freudian; the twenty-first is already Lacanian.

Lacan has not stopped amazing us. Born at the start of the twentieth century, and living through two savage wars, he had begun to acquire fame in the 1930s. But it was between 1950 and 1975 that he exercised his greatest doctrinal authority over French thought. These were years when France, dominated by a social and political ideal inherited from the two movements that grew out of the Resistance – Gaullism and Communism, then by decolonization, and finally by the caesura of May 1968, experienced itself as the most cultured country in the world, a nation where intellectuals occupied a leading position in a *Rechtsstaat* marked by the cult of a universalistic, egalitarian Republic.

In this context, aspirations based on reason and progress were the order of the day – in particular, the project of collectively improving the lot of those affected by mental health problems: neurotics, psychotics, depressives, criminals. And it was precisely then that Lacan insisted that Freud's advances were the sole possible horizon of democratic societies, the only resource capable of grasping all facets of human complexity: the worst and best alike. Notwithstanding his strong inclination to pessimism and irony, he did not become a narrow reactionary.

He was also the only psychoanalytical thinker to consider the legacy of Auschwitz in Freudian fashion, mobilizing Greek tragedy as well as the writings of the

Marquis de Sade to evoke its horror. Unlike Lacan, none of Freud's heirs knew how to reinterpret the issue of the death instinct in the light of the Nazi extermination of the Jews. In the absence of this reworking and Lacan's fascination with the cruellest, darkest part of humanity, psychoanalysis in France would have become a pitiful matter of medical psychology, inheritor of Pierre Janet and Théodule Ribot or, worse still, Léon Daudet, Gustave Le Bon or Pierre Debray-Ritzen.

2

FROM VIENNA TO PARIS

As a new ideological configuration took shape with the decline of monarchical sovereignty in the late nineteenth century – based on the fear of crowds, an adherence to the thesis of racial inequality, and a belief in an ideal of science capable of governing populations – Freud's inventiveness was deployed as a new humanism promoting individual liberties and an exploration of the irrational side of human nature.

An enlightened conservative, Freud was convinced that the advent of democracy would signal the victory of civilization over barbarism. Yet as a good pupil of the sombre Enlightenment, he was also persuaded that this victory would never be definitively won and that each age would always be menaced, through human progress itself, with a constant return of its most devastating instincts. In other words, he argued that humanity needed frustration to contain its aggressiveness and sexual instincts, but that frustration made human beings unhappy because, of all living beings, only humans were haunted by a conscious desire for destruction.

Lacan was even more sombre in his approach to human society, and doubtless more marked by the idea of the fragility of democratic regimes, more interested by insanity, crime and mysticism, and finally more tormented. In a word, he was distinguished from Freud's successors, from Melanie Klein to Donald W. Winnicott and many others, by the distance he rapidly took from any conception of psychoanalysis that reduced it to a clinical corpus.

Freud had rejected philosophy, which he unjustly compared to a paranoid intellectual system, and turned to biology, mythology and archaeology. Lacan took the opposite route by reinserting psychoanalysis in the history of philosophy and reintroducing philosophical thinking into the Freudian corpus. Thereafter, he sought to make psychoanalysis an antidote to philosophy, an 'anti-philosophy', by counter-posing the discourse of the master to that of the analyst. He thereby ran the risk of joining the reactionaries of obscurantism or anti-Enlightenment.[1]

---

1. Traces of it can be found, in particular, in 'L'étourdit' (1973), in *Autres écrits*, Paris, Seuil, 2001, pp. 449–97, and in *Séminaire. Livre XVII, L'Envers de la psychanalyse* (1969–70), ed. Jacques-Alain Miller, Paris, Seuil, 1991. See also Alain Badiou, 'Anti-Philosophy: Plato and Lacan', in *Conditions*, trans. Steve Corcoran, London, Continuum, 2008; Colette Soler, 'Lacan en antiphilosophe', *Filozofski*, vol. XXXVII, no. 2, 2006, pp. 121–44; and Alain Badiou, seminar on Lacan, École normale supérieure, 1994–95.

To be sure, Lacan was a psychiatrist and therefore a clinician, but he could have become something else, even if (as is often forgotten) he had a genuine vocation for public medicine. Moreover, he never left the Saint-Anne Hospital: 'my walls', he used to say, when claiming to 'speak to the walls' (preach in the desert), suffering from not being properly understood. He was an intern there and then a lecturer, before engaging, over and above what was reasonable, in the ritual of the presentation of patients. And that was how he acquired real popularity with thousands of psychologists and mental health workers. Had he not conferred increased prestige on the themes of the founders of institutional psychotherapy, born at the heart of the Resistance in the Saint-Alban Hospital in Lozère, who had promoted a mental health medicine serving patients and no longer subject to the archaic classifications derived from the old asylum order?

During the First World War, as a pupil at the Collège Stanislas, Lacan thought of embarking on a political career, happily regarding himself as a twentieth-century Rastignac. He was interested in everything: new litera-ture, the work of James Joyce, Maurras' style, Léon Bloy's desperate imprecations, libertinism, extreme experiences, the philosophy of Nietzsche. And he had a horror of his family origins: a bigoted mother, a father who was a sales rep crushed by the omnipotence of his own father, and ancestors who were vinegar merchants. In a sense, he rejected the chauvinistic *France profonde* from which he hailed. Hence his attraction to Parisian intellectual elites, avant-garde movements (Dadaism and surrealism), sartorial eccentricity, unusual food, the centres of European culture (London and Rome), and, finally, women who did not resemble his mother, who were not 'maternal'. With women he liked, Lacan always proved extremely generous.[2]

Lacan was his own mother, his own father, his own progenitor, hence desirous of possessing things and beings. He loved lists, collections, unpublished texts and rare editions. This great theorist of the object relation, the necessity of lack, and promotion of the symbolic function of the father, spent his life thinking against himself – against his difficulty in being a father, against the anxiety of lack, against his detestation of mothers. He often dreamed of what he would have liked to be: a text, a woman, a poet, an artist, a clown, a holy man, or Solomon, son of David, famous for his wisdom and for having led the people of Israel to the height of their power.

As a psychoanalyst and head of a school, he was also a mother for his male followers and a father for his female pupils. He could neither abandon them, nor love them for themselves, nor be deserted by anyone without going into a crisis of rage and bitter disappointment as soon as he had to choose one party against another. Lacan was an adventurer in his century, a Sartrean hero, certainly, but even more a Balzacian character,

---

2. All the evidence concurs on this, particularly that which I have been able to gather from Monique Lévi-Strauss, Madeleine Chapsal, Jenny Aubry, Françoise Giroud and Marie-Pierre de Cossé Brissac.

dreaming of living in the old world of the Ancien Régime nobility, the world of Saint-Simon and La Rochefoucauld.

Neither Hugo, nor Dumas, nor even Flaubert: Lacan wrote against the novelistic literature of the nineteenth century. Yet his story was the story of a Balzacian destiny transposed to the twentieth century and, by the same token, repressed. I repeat: Lacan's story is the youth of Louis Lambert, the maturity of Horace Bianchon, the old age of Balthazar Claës. The first succumbed to madness after passing from the most elevated idealism to the most intense sensualism. The second was an admirable doctor of the soul and body, threatened by the rebellion of his desires, indulgent towards others, but hard on himself. The third let himself be carried away by a greed for knowledge that led to his self-destruction.

Like the first, Lacan could have fallen into vagrancy had he not proved able, through his initiation into psychiatric knowledge, to confront insanity – the part of himself that referred him to a tormented family genealogy: a brother, Marc-François, who had chosen monastic confinement; a mother, Émilie, who would never know the man he had become; a father, Alfred, who wanted to make him a mustard merchant.

Like the second, his glory reached a peak at a crucial moment of his existence, between 1950 and 1970, because he believed that the post-Shoah world had repressed the essence of the psychoanalytic revolution and that only a method capable of accounting for unconscious structures – those inscribed in myths and language – could restore it. Following Freud and Adorno, and basing himself on the works of Claude Lévi-Strauss, Lacan wished to enrol himself in an intellectual tradition that enabled him, throughout a sumptuous oeuvre, to free human beings from the universe of the occult, at the risk of dramatizing the powerlessness of reason and truth to accomplish this liberation. And to conclude, he never stopped tragically confronting the issue of death and bodily decline: 'I speak with my body', he often said, 'and this without knowing it. I therefore always say more than I know.' And again: 'Life thinks only of resting as much as possible while awaiting death. Life thinks only of dying.'

Finally, like the third, in the last ten years of his life he succumbed to the temptation of absolute knowledge, believing that in knots and plaits or in mathemes he had discovered a logical-topological model capable of bringing out what speech does not say or, conversely, saying what the unconscious cannot say. Sunk in silence, or now expressing himself solely with the aid of puns, allographs, portmanteau words or neologisms[3] – *Jules Lacue, jaclaque, affreud, ajoyce, l'Aimée de Mathèse*, and so on – he began to resemble old Oedipus, the fallen, blinded tyrant exiled to Colonus and cursing his descendants.[4]

---

3. Marcel Bénabou, Laurent Cornaz, Dominique de Liège and Yan Pélissier, *789 néologismes de Jacques Lacan*, Paris, EPEL, 2002. See Chapter 13 below, 'Places, Books, Objects'.
    4. See Chapter 14, 'Antigone'.

How are we to define the specificity of this complex oeuvre for today's readers and for those who will come after us? I would first of all say that, notwithstanding appearances and the fact that it never exhibits the characteristics of a written, finished oeuvre, it unfolds like an intellectual system in the sense that it possesses an internal coherence based on the invention of rigorous concepts and borrowings from other disciplines: linguistics, philosophy, anthropology, mathematics, and so forth.

It is therefore open to contradictory interpretations, like the texts of literary modernism: an open system, then, even if it is frequently hermetic. Evidence of this is the fact that Lacan never wanted to give the books he published in his lifetime a real title. When it came to collecting his articles in 1966, he entitled the volume *Écrits*; when he published the transcription of his interview for Belgian television in 1970, he chose *Radiophonie*; and similarly, in 1974 he entitled the film in which he was the sole actor *Télévision*.[5] His seminar was published as *Le Séminaire* and when, in 1968, he created a review, he decided that articles in it would appear without the author's name. He called it *Scilicet* ('evidently') and subtitled it 'You are permitted to know what the École freudienne de Paris thinks'. He was its master, the only one to print his name in it; and it was

---

5. *Radiophonie* is an interview with Robert Georgin and *Télévision* is the synopsis of a film by Benoît Jacquot. Both texts are collected in *Autres écrits*, Paris, Seuil, 2001. In English see Jacques Lacan, *Television*, trans. Denis Hollier, Rosalind Krauss and Annette Michelson, New York, Norton, 1990.

the organ of his school, consequently destined to disappear with it and him. Each work was ultimately indicated only as a summary, referred to with an inexhaustible literalism. A minimalist sketch: reference to Mallarmé for the dream of a 'midnight disappeared into itself' (*Igitur*); to Joyce for smashing up the language system; to Francis Ponge for siding with things.

So Lacan was the sole heir of Freud to endow his oeuvre with a philosophical armature and release it from its biological anchorage without lapsing into spiritualism in the process. The paradox of this interpretation is that it reintroduced into psychoanalysis the German philosophical thought from which Freud had distanced himself. This contribution, which he subsequently sought to cancel by designating himself an anti-philosopher, made Lacan the sole master of psychoanalysis in France, which earned him a good deal of hostility. But if some of his fierce detractors were unjust, he laid himself open to criticism by surrounding himself with epigones, who helped obscure his teaching with their jargon. Worse still, he could not do without them, even though he constantly disavowed them by advising them not to imitate him.

3

THE CHILD IN THE MIRROR

Lacan was fascinated by primatology, by stories of rats shut up in labyrinths, by monkeys and zoos. He loved birds, frogs, fish, the noises animals make, bestiaries, plants. Above all, however, he treasured his dog – a female boxer, to whom he attributed romantic feelings for him. 'She lets herself go into transports of passion over my person', he said, 'in which she assumes an utterly formidable aspect for the most timorous souls, such as exist, for example, among my offspring. People are afraid that when she begins to jump all over me, flattening her ears and growling in a certain way, the fact that she takes my wrists between her teeth might be taken for a threat. But it's nothing of the sort. She loves me and a few words from me restore everything to order . . . She never takes me for someone else.'[1]

---

1. Jacques Lacan, *Le Séminaire. Livre IX, L'Identification*

As Darwinian as Freud, Lacan nevertheless remained attached to a certain naturalism – that of Buffon – revised and corrected by the surrealist painters, who were themselves immersed in the universe of African mythography. Lacan's prose reminds one of certain paintings by Giorgio De Chirico or Salvador Dali, his old friend and accomplice, but above all, and amazingly, those by René Magritte.

Perilous and polished, this prose examines the discrepancy between the object and its representation, while reducing reality to a wild irruption shot through with formulae and arabesques. According to Lacan, any reality must be stated in an objective fashion, without the slightest lyricism, for every reality is first of all a real – that is, a hallucination. Lacan describes reality as would a painter whose model is an egg placed on the table, but who draws a bird unfurling large wings on his canvas. He associates beings and things, landscapes and words, bodies and faces, mirrors and children.

It was in 1936 that Lacan began to be initiated into Hegelian philosophy, participating with Raymond Queneau, Georges Bataille and many others in Alexandre Kojève's seminar on the *Phenomenology of Spirit*, which led him to develop his conception of the subject and the imaginary. The same year, he gave a famous lecture on the mirror stage to the 14th Congress of the International Psychoanalytical Association (IPA) in Marienbad, thus

---

(1961–62), unpublished, transcribed by Michel Roussan; session of 29 November 1961.

making his meteoric entrée onto the stage of the international psychoanalytical movement. In it he told the story of a child placed before a mirror who, unlike a monkey, rejoiced at the sight of its image. The intervention lasted ten minutes: a short session *avant la lettre*. As for the text, no one has succeeded in finding a trace of it. The IPA's great organizer, Ernest Jones, fulminated that day against this French speaker, whom he had never heard speak, and who did not stick to the allotted time. Humiliated, Lacan left the congress and went to the Berlin Olympic Games. The spectacle of that ceremony was to haunt him all his life.

Two years later, he included the content of his lecture in an article on the family commissioned by Henri Wallon for the *Encyclopédie française* (1938). The introduction – 'Mirror Stage' – contained two parts: 'Second Power of the Mirror Image' and 'Narcissistic Structure of the Ego'. It was precisely from Wallon, a Communist psychologist and Hegelian, that he borrowed this terminology. Always quick to erase the original archive, Lacan neglected to cite his source. Subsequently, he always suppressed Wallon's name and presented himself as the inventor of the term.

Yet he was influenced less by Wallon than Kojève, who suggested that the modern thought of the 1930s should register a new revolution: the transition from a philosophy of *I think* (Descartes) to a philosophy of *I desire* (Freud, Hegel). In other words, following Kojève, Lacan conceived the other or otherness as the object of a desiring consciousness.

Wallon had used the term 'mirror test' to refer to an experiment wherein a child, placed in front of a mirror, gradually succeeds in distinguishing its 'own body' from its reflected image. According to him, this dialectical operation was accomplished thanks to a symbolic understanding by the subject of the imaginary space in which its unity was fashioned. From Wallon's perspective, the mirror test referred to the transition from the specular to the imaginary and then from the imaginary to the symbolic.

Like some surrealist painter, Lacan adopted Wallon's terminology only to transform the 'mirror test' into a 'mirror stage' – that is, into an admixture of two concepts: the intra-psychic position, in Melanie Klein's sense, and the stage (evolution), in Freud's sense. Thus he made any reference to a natural dialectic disappear. From Lacan's perspective, the mirror stage became a psychic, even ontological, operation, whereby the human being is constituted in an identification with her fellow.

Like Melanie Klein, Lacan took up Freud's second topography – ego, id, super-ego – in contradistinction to any ego psychology. Two options were possible from 1923 onwards. The first consisted in making the ego the product of a gradual differentiation from the id, acting as representative of reality and responsible for containing the instincts (such was the ego psychology of the American school). By contrast, the second turned its back on any idea of the autonomy of the ego in order to study its genesis in terms of identification (this was the option of the French school).

According to Lacan, who borrowed the idea from Louis Bolk, a Dutch embryologist, the significance of the mirror stage was bound up with the prematurity of birth indicated by the anatomic incompletion of the pyramidal system and the lack of motor coordination in the early months of life. Henceforth, and increasingly over the years, Lacan distanced himself from a psychological optic, describing the process from the angle of the unconscious. He thereby came to argue that the specular world, site of the primordial identity of the ego, contains no otherness. Hence the canonical definition: the mirror stage is a phase – that is, a state which, as a structure, succeeds another state, and not a stage in the evolutionistic sense of the word.

Just as Freud had separated himself from neurology by showing that the imaginary topography of the body – fantasy – never coincides with a real anatomy or neuronal trace, so Lacan invented a mirror stage that had no need of the prop of a stage or a real mirror.

Urged to return to the International Psychoanalytical Association and avenge the humiliation he had suffered, Lacan gave a second lecture on the mirror stage in Zurich in 1949. There he once again met Ernest Jones, who this time allowed him time to read his paper. He had asked his friend Monique Lévi-Strauss to type his manuscript, which she gladly did. And when she experienced some difficulty in understanding what he meant, he provided her with enlightening explanations while stressing that his inspiration came from Mallarmé's prose.

Rather than speaking about the stage or mirror, or objects discrepant with their representation, in Zurich Lacan engaged in a vast reflection on the notion of the subject in psychoanalysis and the history of science. Hence his adoption of a much longer title: 'The Mirror Stage as Formative of the *I* Function as Revealed in Psychoanalytical Experience'.[2]

2. See Jacques Lacan, *Écrits*, trans. Bruce Fink, New York, Norton, 2007, Chapter 5. Cf. Élisabeth Roudinesco, 'The Mirror Stage: An Obliterated Archive', in Jean-Michel Rabaté, ed., *The Cambridge Companion to Lacan*, Cambridge, Cambridge University Press, 2003.

4

THE SUBJECT REINVENTED

During the summer of 1936 – the season of the first paid holidays in France – Lacan spent his vacation with his first wife, Marie-Louise Blondin, who was five months pregnant. Aged thirty-five, about to face the novel trial of fatherhood, he wrote a programmatic article, 'Beyond the "Reality Principle"', in which he heralded the advent of a new generation of Freudians. Regarding himself as their leader, he assigned them the task of 'reading Freud' against, and to the exclusion of, any ego psychology.

This summons to rebellion was an extension of Lacan's initial version of the mirror stage. Amid the triumph of the reforms introduced by the Popular Front, he once more seemed to be going against the ideals of his times by distancing himself from the idea that the individual could adapt to reality or seek to transform it. He made mental identification a constitutive form of human knowledge, proposing the term 'imaginary posts of the personality' for the three instances of Freud's second topographical model, so as to free it from it a fourth – the 'I' – to which he allocated a precise role: being the place where a subject can recognize itself, in an imaginary fashion, as a subject.

In 1949 Lacan thus no longer held the same positions as he had before the war. Not only did he draw on the work of Melanie Klein and Claude Lévi-Strauss, but he took on board the principles of Ferdinand de Saussure's linguistics, thus passing from an existential representation of the subject based on phenomenology to a structural conception of subjectivity, wherein the subject is above all immersed in language – that is, in a symbolic function that determines it unawares. Furthermore, he proceeded to a highly stimulating reading of the Cartesian *cogito*.

To understand its significance, we must refer to the lecture he gave at the Bonneval conference of 1946, 'Remarks on Psychic Causality'.[1] In the presence of Henri Ey, who proposed combining neurology

---

1. Immediately after the Second World War, under the guidance of Henri Ey, this conference brought together all the representatives of dynamic, humanist psychiatry. It aimed to redefine the humanist principles of confinement to asylums and the treatment of insanity following the carnage of the Occupation period: 45,000 mentally ill people, abandoned by their families, died of hunger – not (as in Germany) as a result of a decision to exterminate them, but because the large nineteenth-century asylums were no longer capable of feeding them at a time of food shortages. Cf. Isabelle von Bueltzingsloewen, *L'Hécatombe des fous*, Paris, Aubier, 2007.

and psychiatry to ground an organo-dynamic approach to the psyche, Lacan advocated rethinking psychiatric knowledge on the model of the Freudian unconscious. And against the scientists who reduced man to a machine, he shared the conviction with a majority of psychiatrists at the time that psychoanalysis could impart a humanist dimension to psychiatry. Thus, in line with the founders of institutional psychotherapy, he rejected the idea of describing symptoms separately from the subjective lived experience of insanity.[2]

For this reason Lacan advocated a major return to the thought of Descartes – not to a philosophy of the *cogito*, but to a form of thought capable of thinking the causality of insanity. In a few lines he commented on a sentence from the first of the *Meditations* that subsequently formed the focus of a famous dispute between Michel Foucault and Jacques Derrida:[3]

Again, these hands, and my whole body – how can their existence be denied? Unless indeed I likened myself to some lunatics, whose brains are so upset by persistent

2. Something that is the case today with the security-minded and biological-behavioural descriptions that have invaded psychiatric discourse via the various versions of the *Diagnostic and Statistical Manual of Mental Disorders* (DSM).

3. Jacques Derrida, 'Cogito and the History of Madness', in *Writing and Difference*, trans. Alan Bass, London, Routledge and Kegan Paul, 1978, Chapter 2, and Michel Foucault, *History of Madness*, ed. Jean Khalfa, trans. Jonathan Murphy and Jean Khalfa, New York, Routledge, 2006.

melancholy vapours that they firmly assert that they are
kings, when really they are miserably poor; or that they
are clad in purple, when really they are naked; or that
they have a head of pottery, or are pumpkins, or are
made of glass; but then they are madmen, and I should
appear no less mad if I took them as a precedent for my
own case.[4]

In 1949 Lacan thus let it be understood (as, later, would
Derrida) that Descartes' foundation of modern thought
did not exclude the phenomenon of madness.

If we compare this position with that of 1949 on the
mirror stage, we see that Lacan had changed perspec-
tives. Having invoked Descartes in 1946, he now
rejected Cartesianism, stressing that the experience of
psychoanalysis was 'radically opposed to any philosophy derived from the *cogito*'. In the 1966 version – the
one published in *Écrits* – he corrected his lecture by
strengthening his critique of Cartesianism: psychoanalysis, he asserted, 'is opposed to any philosophy
directly derived from the *cogito*'.

We can therefore clearly see how Lacan developed
between 1936 and 1949. Initially, he developed a
phenomenological theory of the imaginary and a surrealist theory of the object, while distancing himself from
the biological notion of stage. Next he invoked Cartesian
rationality to show that insanity possesses its own logic

---

4. Descartes, *Philosophical Writings*, trans. and ed. Elizabeth
Anscombe and Peter Thomas Geach, London, Nelson's University
Paperbacks/Open University Press, 1975, p. 62.

and cannot be conceived outside of the *cogito*. Thirdly, and finally, he invented a theory of the subject that rejects not the Cartesian *cogito*, but a tradition of ego psychology derived from the *cogito*.[5]

5. All these texts were collected by François Wahl in Lacan's *Écrits*. See Chapter 11, '1966: The *Écrits*'.

FAMILIES, I LOVE YOU, I HATE YOU

This reflection on the subject, the stage, the mirror, the discrepant object, the *cogito* and insanity would be nothing if, in addition to basing himself on phenomenology and then structuralism and Saussurean linguistics, Lacan had not from 1938 onwards taken account of the anthropological development of the western family. For psychoanalysis as a discipline could not dispense with reflection on this issue in as much as Freud, with his return to the grand narratives featuring the royal dynasties of ancient Greece, had inscribed his approach in the long history of the transformation of relations within the bourgeois family: the rebellion of sons against fathers, the desire to control – no longer to repress – infantile sexuality, perversion, homosexuality and, finally, femininity in all its forms.

It was in a text subsequently entitled 'Family Complexes in the Formation of the Individual' that

Lacan offered a synthesis of the state of the family on the eve of the Second World War.[1] Here he blended clinical and psychopathological considerations with an analysis of different psychoanalytical, anthropological and sociological theories, in order to understand the status and evolution of the family.

Combining the theses of Louis de Bonald with those of Aristotle and Émile Durkheim, he also drew inspiration from the German biologist Jakob von Uexküll, who had revolutionized the study of animal and human behaviour by showing that environmental belonging must be conceived as the internalization of this environment in the lived experience of each species. Armed with these references, Lacan drew a crepuscular picture of the modern nuclear family, showing that the subject's anchorage in an environment should not be construed as a contract between a free individual and a society, but as a relationship of dependency between an environment and an individual determined by specific acts of internalization of elements of that environment.

Lacan stressed that the family was organized as a set of unconscious representations – or imagos – marked by the two poles of the paternal and the maternal. Outside of this affiliation, which according to Lacan characterized the socially organic character of the family, no humanization of the individual was possible.

---

1. Jacques Lacan, 'Les complexes familiaux dans la formation de l'individu', in *Autres écrits*, Paris, Seuil, 2001, pp. 23–84.

Lacan seemingly regarded the family as an organic whole and had no hesitation in castigating the decline of the paternal imago which, in his view, was so characteristic of the disastrous state of European society in the late 1930s. However, contrary to the theorists of Counter-Revolution, he was opposed to the idea that a restoration of patriarchal omnipotence represented a solution to the problem. Similarly, he refused to make the family the crux of any perpetuation of the race, territory or heredity. Convinced that the old sovereignty of the father was gone for good, he maintained that any attempt at restoration could only result in a caricature, an artifice, even fascism with its dangerous military parades. But by the same token he also rejected all libertarian, hedonist or Communist pretensions to abolish the family. Neither restoration of the virility of the father converted into an authoritarian boss, nor dissolution of the family model into a collective that claimed to be a substitute for it.

Lacan learnt the lesson of Freud's gesture. The revalorization of a father 'deconstructed' by the end of monarchical sovereignty could be nothing but symbolic. Basing himself on Henri Bergson, who in 1932 had opposed an ethics of obligation to an ethics of aspiration, Lacan regarded the proscription of the mother as the concrete form of a primordial obligation or an enclosed ethics. The weaning or separation complex was its expression, because it restored the interrupted nourishing relationship in the form of an 'imago of the female breast'. The existence of this imago, Lacan maintained, dominates the whole of human life like some appeal to a nostalgia for the whole. But when this imago is not sublimated to enable access to the social bond, it becomes deadly as it becomes fusional. Hence a desire for death, which the subject can exhibit in the form of suicidal behaviour. In contrast, Lacan situated the function of aspiration and openness in a separating authority, represented by the paternal pole.

Crucible of violence, madness and neurosis, in Lacan's view the family was therefore the worst of structures – with the exception of all the others. Thus he rendered homage to Freud:

> The sublime accident of genius is possibly not the only explanation of the fact that it was in Vienna – at the time capital of a state which was the melting-pot of the most varied family forms, from the most archaic to the most developed, from the latest agnatic groupings of Slav peasants, via feudal or mercantile paternalisms, to the narrowest forms of petit-bourgeois domesticity and the most decadent forms of the unstable ménage – that a son of the Jewish patriarchy invented the Oedipus complex. Be that as it may, the forms of neurosis dominant at the end of the last century revealed that they were profoundly dependent on family conditions.[2]

Like Freud, Lacan defended the values of an enlightened conservatism, while relying on the theses of modern

2. Ibid., p. 61.

anthropology[3] to demonstrate that Freudianism served as a rampart both against attempts to abolish the family and aspirations to restore the authoritarian figure of a masquerade of chiefdom.

For my part, I have always thought that psychoanalysis was born in a social context marked by the decline of patriarchal power and the development of a universalistic form of thought articulated by the Jews of the *Haskalah*, who rejected the very idea that there could be such a thing as 'Jewish science' or a 'Jewish outlook' on the world. And that is why the history of psychoanalysis cannot be written without a reflection on the Jewish question. Only a form of thought capable of desacralizing communitarian anchorage could yield the invention of psychoanalysis – a discipline that knows neither territory, nor nation, nor borders.

In Freud's era the 'declinist' thesis was expressed in forms other than those we see flourishing today. We encounter it in various late-nineteenth-century thinkers and writers, from Richard Wagner, via Jakob Bachofen, to August Strindberg. But far from seeking to restore this deposed figure, as do the perennial nostalgists of 'things were better in the past', Freud had registered it, becoming attached to the fate of two tragic heroes: Oedipus, on the one hand, and Hamlet on the other – the one embodying the immutability of the unconscious, the other the guilty conscience.[4]

---

3. Only later would he draw on the work of Claude Lévi-Strauss.
4. See Chapter 14, 'Antigone'.

Hence a dual dynamic in his thought: psychoanalysis was indeed engendered by the questions prompted by the decline of patriarchy, but it sought to respond to them with a new conception of the family, wherein the father's place was redefined.

In 1976 Michel Foucault registered what Lacan had already perceived and drew a political conclusion that has always seemed to me highly pertinent. In its essence, he argued, not only is psychoanalysis in theoretical and political opposition to fascism – even if its practitioners are not.[5] In providing sexuality with a law, and demarcating itself from the racism of theories of inequality, it has also had the merit of distrusting all procedures for controlling and managing everyday sexuality. In short, Foucault attributed a 'political honour' to psychoanalysis as a discipline, and to Freud's invention a capacity for exposing the mechanisms of the dominant power by means of doubt. He also asserted that it was contemporary with laws on loss of paternal authority. Indeed, when in Vienna Freud listened to the complaints by one or another of his hysterical patients against her father, the figure of the latter was as much elevated into an object of love within the bourgeois family as he was condemned by the law if incestuous or violent towards his children.[6]

In this respect, Lacan was not, as some people think today, the supporter of a view of the family restricted to

5. We should not forget that numerous psychoanalysts have collaborated with the worst political regimes – Nazism, fascism and Latin American dictatorships.

6. Michel Foucault, *The History of Sexuality*, Vol. 1, trans. Robert Hurley, London, Allen Lane, 1979, p. 130.

the primacy of a biological difference between the sexes that makes woman a being inferior to man. While he argued that every subject is subjected to the symbolic Law, that law in no way resembles a reactionary phallus elevated into a policeman's truncheon.

Lacan's conception does not a priori prohibit parental positions being occupied by persons of the same sex. And while in 1938 Lacan could not imagine what the fate of the family would be sixty years later, he nevertheless predicted a radiant future for it, on account of its capacity to generate and integrate the normal and the pathological, the rule and deviation, Law and transgression of the Law.

Lacan spent the whole of the Occupation dealing with family affairs. His marriage was based on a misunderstanding. Marie-Louis Blondin believed she was marrying a perfect man whose conjugal fidelity would match her dreams of happiness. But Lacan was not such a man, and never would be. Three children were born of their union: Caroline, Thibault and Sibylle. In 1937 Lacan fell in love with Sylvia Bataille, the actress in *Partie de campagne*,[7] separated that year from Georges Bataille.

In September 1940 Lacan found himself in an impossible situation, obliged to tell his legitimate wife, who was eight months pregnant by him, that his companion was also expecting a child. A Jew of Romanian origin, Sylvia had taken refuge in the unoccupied zone to escape

---

7. Directed by Jean Renoir, 1936.

deportation. Lacan subsequently concealed from the offspring of his first marriage bed the existence of his daughter Judith, born under the name of Bataille, to whom he could only transmit his family name in 1964. This was the fertile ground on which he developed the theory of the Name-of-the-Father, sketched in 1953 and finalized three years later, to refer to the signifier of the paternal role. Being the embodiment of the signifier because he calls the child by his name, the father intervenes with the child as depriver of the mother. In other words, Lacan once again asserted that the family is at the base of human societies solely because it is dominated by the primacy of language: naming, he argued, enables a subject to acquire an identity.

Whenever Lacan wanted to lambast his opponents – and hence ridiculous fathers and their valets (like the IPA, re-baptized the Interfamilial Analytic Association) – he would not deny himself the opportunity of adding further neologisms to 'his' Name-of-the-Father (*Nom-du-père*). Transition from the singular to the plural, suppression of capital letters or hyphens, phonic reformulations – the terminology on this theme became luxuriant. Thus: 'It is in the kingdom of the dead that the *non-dupes errent*' [non-dupes wander]; or, 'But it is a name to lose like the others, to drop in perpetuity! The names of the father, what, the *anôns* [donkey foals] of the father, what a pack!'[8] And, why not?, *père-Orang, père-vers, ânons du*

---

8. Marcel Bénabou, Laurent Cornaz, Dominique de Liège and Yan Pélissier, *789 néologismes de Jacques Lacan*, Paris, EPEL, 2002, pp. 64–5.

*père, père-versement, père-version, permaître, père-
ternité,* and so on. Lacan felt sorry for fathers and hated
mothers and families, while himself being an actor in the
intra-familial humiliations he denounced.

While not participating in the Resistance, Lacan
clearly manifested his hostility to all forms of anti-
Semitism and racism. He loathed anything closely or
remotely connected with collaboration. This has not
stopped radical anti-Lacanians from making him a
collaborator, a supporter of Vichy and a Pétainist, even
an anti-Semite; and idolatrous Lacanians from inventing
a heroic past in the Resistance for him. One of them
even went so far as to imagine that Lacan was Jewish
and that, under his assumed name, he was concealing
his true identity: Lacanovitch. This is a pernicious thesis,
since it seeks to reactivate the idea that psychoanalysis is
a 'Jewish science' whose renewal could be undertaken
exclusively by a Jew.[9]

In September 1945 Lacan went to England to study
the 'small group' experiment conducted by John
Rickman and Wilfred Ruprecht Bion, which sought to
facilitate reclassification of offenders in the army. On
his return, in a lecture on British psychiatry he lauded
the merits of this adaptive model, which he had consist-
ently criticized. It was better to promote identification
with the collective ideal, he said, than to train the individual to imitate bosses.

9. This is a thesis I have refuted, particularly in *Retour sur la
question juive* (Paris, Albin Michel, 2009), but which, alas, persists in
the minds of staunch communitarians.

Passing from reflections on the family to comments on the social and psychic functioning of collectives, Lacan ultimately developed a theory of freedom opposed to that of Sartrean existentialism. Indeed, according to him, hell is not other people, since access to identity always presupposes a relationship to others mediated by the Law. Far from being the result of a conscious decision, freedom thus pertains to an imperative logic, unconscious in kind, which alone can break the subject's adhesion to the imago of its servitude. In other words, in order to be free, it is necessary to be capable of assessing the determinations imposed on subjectivity by the unconscious.

Twenty-five years later, extending his reflection on the question of groups and freedom, Lacan constructed his theory of the four discourses: of the master, possessor of the attributes of tyranny; of the hysteric, trustee of a failed rebellion; of the university, inheritor of academic knowledge. To these he counter-posed psychoanalytic discourse, which in his view was the only one capable of replacing the others, by destroying them. Psychoanalysis was once again allocated a subversive role.

Borrowing the notion of surplus-value from Marx, Lacan showed that its psychic equivalent was 'surplus-*jouissance*' – another neologism. From it he deduced that, while emancipation is worthwhile, it can never be unlimited, on pain of drowning desire in the dark continent of a boundless libertarian disaster, a surplus-*jouissance* eluding all symbolization. Then, in highly pragmatic fashion, he applied his theory of the four discourses to the events of May 1968, with the immediate aim of getting those of his followers who had strayed into a political engagement he deemed extremist and ridiculous – Maoism – to return to psychoanalysis.

In a flight of fancy inherited from Kojève, Lacan maintained that revolution always ends in the recreation of a more tyrannical master than the one whose regime it has abolished. Worse still, if people were not careful, revolution risked being based on a science elevated into a religion and issuing in a world from which any form of subjectivity was banished.[10]

For the youth of the 1960s and '70s Lacan was a consciousness raiser: he rehabilitated the desire for revolution, while seeking to be the guarantor of a law that would punish its excesses.

Commenting on this political stance, in 1981 Michel Foucault stressed how far Sartre and Lacan might be regarded as 'alternating contemporaries'.[11] I adopted this assessment because I was so struck, when studying with Gilles Deleuze and Michel de Certeau, by the way that from 1943 onwards the theoretical and political situation of these two masters of freedom had constantly intersected, conflicted, or clashed, without them ever meeting one another. Both of them – the first like an elder brother, the second like a strict father – helped the

---

10. Jacques Lacan, *Le Séminaire. Livre XVII, L'Envers de la psychanalyse* (1969–70), Paris, Seuil, 1991.

11. See Élisabeth Roudinesco, *Histoire de la psychoanalyse en France/Jacques Lacan*, Paris, Le Livre de Poche, 2009, p. 1900.

Maoist youth post–May 1968 not to turn to terrorism. This statement of the obvious will not prevent detractors of Lacan and Sartre from comparing them to raging dictators hostile to democracy and inciting their followers to plant bombs.

6

LOVING MARGUERITE

Like virtually all doctors of the human soul, Lacan owed his initial fame to a woman, to a case, to the existence of an insane woman – Marguerite Anzieu – whom he nicknamed Aimée in his medical thesis, defended in 1932.

We know that behind the case histories narrated by the masters there lies, like a palimpsest, the anonymous, mute story of the subjects who enabled them to fashion their doctrines.

Their tragic lives have been explored by science, as have those, even more terrifying, of the abnormal, the monsters or the so-called 'inferior races', exhibited in fairs in the early nineteenth century and then coldly observed by men of science: Georges Cuvier, Étienne Geoffroy Saint-Hilaire, Jean-Étienne Esquirol, Franz Joseff Gall, and many others. Women are always in a majority in the land of the 'case' people, from

Anne-Josèphe Théroigne de Méricourt to the 'Hottentot Venus', but we also encounter a number of perverts, criminals, lunatics, homosexuals, and 'masturbating' children. In short, a whole population that was thought to be 'different' – or unfit for procreation – and to embody (why not?) the missing link between man and the animals, but also between rational man and his bestial other side. A difference elevated into something universal: on the one hand, a politics of things based on observation and evaluation; on the other, a universe of subjects condemned to be 'ranked' in accordance with an ideal of fixity.

While we are indebted to Darwin for demolishing the thesis of the missing link, supposed to connect the negro with the monkey so as to exclude the civilized white man from the animal kingdom, we are indebted to Freud, following the Marquis de Puységur, for being the first to overturn the hierarchy that accorded a monopoly on speech to the master, the only one empowered to translate the discourse of the subject under observation. The irruption of speech – and hence of women's speech – onto the scene of a new science of the psyche was doubtless one of the founding moments in the history of Freudianism.

Now of course, Freud and his heirs gave a voice to the subject listened to – and no longer observed – solely in order to adduce evidence, elusive in terms of assessment, of the truth of a theory and the effectiveness of a form of therapy. Consequently, they left to historians the task of deconstructing the mythical power of case notes and replacing (without ever erasing) them by the true history of the real patient concealed behind the scientific fiction – to the extent that it is now accepted that lifting the anonymity of cases underpins any form of serious historiography in this area. Likewise, the lifting of anonymity is about to become established in sperm donation procedures, as if a knowledge of biological origin were as crucial for a subject as the disclosure of a hitherto-effaced archive.

While the therapist reconstructs a fiction intended to prove the validity of his theses, the patient for her part seeks to know whether what she has lived through is positive or negative. And to convey her experience, she resorts to a practice of self-writing that expresses a quite different view from the one sought by the therapist. As for the restoration by historians of the reality of the therapy, it makes it possible to give a voice to beings without writing, whose traces have been discovered in the archives.

All these narrative structures are distinct from one another, but in their coexistence they attest in every age to an incessant division between a critical consciousness (that of scholars and historians) and a lived consciousness (that of witnesses).

Today, it is virtually impossible to write major case histories. Indeed, for thirty years novelists have massively invested the technique of therapy, either because they are faced with it as patients, or because they have supplanted psychoanalysts by becoming the narrators of their ego-story. Auto-fiction, which promotes a narrative 'freed from internal censorship',[1] while being based on the principle of a correspondence between narrator, author and hero, has replaced the descriptive formalism issued from the *Nouveau roman*,[2] which was devoid of plot, subjectivity and psychology, to the extent that every novelistic work now resembles a case history.

With authors now no longer submitting to the rules of an aestheticization capable of transforming some reality into a narrative distanced from emotion – in line with the legacy of Marcel Proust, Philip Roth or Serge Doubrovsky – the contemporary practice of auto-fiction has ended up reducing literature to the dramatization of putative authenticity, sex and emotion: a kind of autobiography making it possible for an author to take herself for the clinician of her own pathology.

Furthermore, at the same time as the cult of auto-fiction was developing, patients, thanks to television, the internet and mass communication, have been transformed into confessors of their own neurosis. Therewith psychoanalysts found themselves as if stripped of their status as commentators on cases – all the more so in that these same patients have won the power to take legal action against their therapists when they recognize

---

1. In 1977 the writer Serge Doubrovsky coined this neologism in his novel *Fils* (Paris, Galilée), to refer to a literary genre defined by a pact combining two kinds of narration: autobiography and fiction. It therefore involves a cross between a real narrative of the author's life and a fictional narrative exploring an experience lived by the latter.
2. A term used from 1957 onwards to refer to the literary school of Alain Robbe-Grillet, Nathalie Sarraute and Claude Simon.

themselves in the narrative therapists construct of their treatment and it does not suit them.

The ancestral division between critical consciousness and lived consciousness thus seems to have disappeared from our horizon as the trust reposed by the subject in the representative of the care institution has vanished. As a result, contemporary psychoanalysts have abandoned the major medical histories that were once standard in the scientific community, in favour of case micro-narratives intended to illustrate some particular aspect of a clinical orientation.

I never met Marguerite Anzieu. Courtesy, however, of her son Didier, I have been able to reconstruct her story, which, although highly singular, is nevertheless similar to that of other madwomen who enabled certain masters of psychoanalysis to develop their clinical theories.[3]

Hailing like Lacan from a Catholic and landed milieu, she was raised by a mother who suffered from persecution symptoms. In the fashion of a modern Emma Bovary, very early on she dreamed of becoming something other than what she was: an intellectual and a novelist.

In 1910 she started work in post office administration and, seven years later, married a civil servant. In 1921 she began to exhibit strange behaviour: persecution mania and states of depression. She then settled

---

3. Cf. also Jean Allouch, *Marguerite ou l'Aimée de Lacan*, 2nd revised and expanded edition, Paris, EPEL, 1994.

into a double life: on the one hand, the everyday universe of her post office activities; on the other, an imaginary existence full of hallucinations. In 1930 she wrote two novels in quick succession that she wanted to have published; and convinced herself that she was the victim of attempted persecution by Huguette Duflos, a famous actress on the Parisian stage in the 1930s. In April 1931 she tried to kill Duflos with a knife, but the actress avoided the blow and Marguerite was confined in the Saint-Anne Hospital, where in June 1931 she was entrusted to Lacan, who diagnosed her condition as a case of erotomania and self-punishment paranoia.

Between the psychiatrist and Marguerite there was never the slightest understanding. She had no intention of being treated or looked after; and he did not seek to persuade her to regard herself as a patient. His interest in this woman did not extend beyond illustrating his doctrine of paranoia. For her part, ever the rebel, she refused to be a 'case' and criticized him throughout her life for having wanted to make her into what she was not. This does not mean her interviews with him were negative. And when she left the asylum she ceased, if not to hallucinate, then at least to act in ways that might have been harmful.

A still unpublished manuscript by Marguerite Anzieu, written in Saint-Anne and dated 21 November 1931, reveals that after several months of interviews she was still the same. In this document, which is presented as a kind of auto-anamnesis, she speaks of her childhood, her brothers, her mother and the pain inflicted on her by her relatives, which she did not deserve. And she says she was incapable of defending herself against a family circle that persecuted her. Finally, she complains about having been separated from her son and not being able to raise him as she would have liked. Then she adds: 'Other people's opinions don't affect me in any way, but nothing hurts me more than when I'm told that people have no confidence in me. Everyone says I'm stupid and that's the only thing that lasts.'[4]

Marguerite therefore became famous under the name of Aimée, by the same token ensuring the fame of the person who had written her history, since it allowed him to produce a magnificent synthesis of the clinical theories developed by the psychiatric generation of the 1930s.[5] The book in which she was the heroine was greeted as a literary masterpiece by writers, painters and poets – in particular, by René Crevel, Paul Nizan and Salvador Dali. All of them admired Lacan's use of the patient's novelistic texts and the power of his conception of female insanity. None of them, however, concerned themselves with Marguerite, renamed Aimée.

The rest of the story indicates how far the destiny of the master was bound up with that of his patient. In 1949 Marguerite's son, Didier Anzieu, decided to

---

4. This manuscript forms part of the archives of the Pantaine family. It was confided to me by Julien Bogousslavsky.

5. Jacques Lacan, *De la psychose paranoïaque dans ses rapports avec la personnalité* (1932), Paris, Seuil, 1975. Didier Anzieu, *Une peau pour les pensées. Entretiens avec Gilbert Tarrab*, Paris, Clancier-Guenaud, 1986.

become an analyst and did his training analysis on Lacan's couch. He did not know that his mother was the subject of the famous 'Aimée' case. As for Lacan, he did not recognize this man as the son of the old postal worker. Moreover, he claimed that she had been confined under her maiden name – which was not correct.

Anzieu learnt the truth from his mother's mouth when, in an extraordinary coincidence, she had been placed as a housekeeper in the home of Alfred Lacan, Jacques' father. The conflicts between Didier Anzieu and his analyst were as violent as those that pitted Marguerite against her psychiatrist. Indeed, she criticized Lacan for having treated her as a 'case', not a human being, and for never having returned the manuscripts she had given him during her confinement in Saint-Anne. In her view, Lacan had become what she had dreamed of becoming and, to that end, had robbed her of her most precious possession: her writing. Didier Anzieu never received any response to his requests from Lacan's heirs.[6]

On my side, it was with some sadness that I was to learn in 2011, twelve years after Didier Anzieu's death, that his heirs had sold the archives concerning Marguerite to a specialist bookshop: family photographs, documents and letters exchanged between Didier and several of his correspondents, including mine.[7] Unquestionably,

6. I too have sought in vain to recover these texts.
7. I owe this information to Julien Bogousslavsky, who is today in possession of this file.

some French psychoanalysts – and highly respected ones
at that – have a very strange relationship with their
archives, unlike their English and American counter-
parts, who have long had the habit of donating theirs to
specialist foundations or institutions.[8] This is probably
related to the fact that in the Anglophone world most
analysts are immigrants, or the offspring of immigrants,
and (like the Freud family) have always been concerned
to leave behind traces of their history.

---

8. This is not the case with numerous other French psychoanalysts
– among them, Serge Leclaire, Wladimir Granoff and René Major, who
have entrusted their archives to me.

7

THE ARCHIVE

If everything is filed, monitored, noted or judged, history as creation is no longer possible: it is replaced by the archive transformed into absolute knowledge. But if nothing is filed, if everything is erased or destroyed, then there is nothing to stop narrative being swept off into fantasy, or the hallucinatory sovereignty of the ego, in favour of a kind of archive that functions as a dogma.

Between these two impossibilities, which are like two boundaries of the same prohibition – prohibition of absolute knowledge, prohibition of the interpretative sovereignty of the ego – it must be accepted that archives – destroyed, existing, excessive or erased – are the precondition of history. In other words, blind submission to the positivity of the archive is as certain to result in the impossibility of history-writing as rejection of the archive.

Throughout his life, Lacan behaved ambivalently towards archives.[9] Just as he believed that 'love is giving what you haven't got to someone who doesn't want it', so he thought that the power of archives is all the greater to the extent that they are absent. And that is one of the reasons why his manuscripts, notes and correspondence have not been sorted, inventoried or 'deposited'.

For Lacanian loyalists, it is as if Lacan was himself the guarantor of an already written history in the future anterior. Since no trace is available, this leads to the idea that the oeuvre has no sources, no history, no origin. Similarly, the subject Lacan exists only by hearsay: *bons mots*, rumours, anecdotes. Hence the cult of neologisms: to christen itself, each Lacanian group selects from among the glossary of words invented by the master. Lacan's words – crazy words, bizarre words – then serve to compensate for the missing archives. The cult of the absence of archives corresponds not only to the ideology of Lacanian dogmatism, but also to a certain Lacanian conception of history.

Even though he left his oeuvre in an unfinished state, Lacan attributed exorbitant power to archives – especially written archives. On the one hand, he refused any form of historicization of Freud's thought, seeking to be the interpreter of a new orthodoxy based on a return to Freud's texts. On the other, he was obsessed by a desire for history and the wish to bequeath a written trace of

---

9. Cf. Élisabeth Roudinesco, *L'Analyse, l'archive*, Paris, BNF, 2000.

his teaching and his person – a trace he dreamed of controlling completely.

In other words, Lacan sought to capture the archive in the way that the subject captures its image in the mirror. In 1964, underscoring the extent to which the desire to distinguish the true from the false went hand in hand with a preoccupation with biography in Descartes, Lacan maintained that biography is always secondary with respect to the meaning of an oeuvre.[10] Fifteen years later, he made a sensational statement to the historian Lucile Ritvo during a lecture at Yale University:

> Psychoanalysis has a weight in history. If there are things that belong to it, it is things of the order of psychoanalysis . . . What people call history is the history of epidemics. The Roman Empire, for example, is an epidemic . . . psychoanalysis is an epidemic . . . Without written documents, you know you are in a dream. What the historian requires is a text: a text or a piece of paper. At any rate, somewhere in an archive there must be something that certifies in writing, and whose absence renders history impossible. What cannot be certified in writing cannot be regarded as history.[11]

On the one hand, an assertion of the sovereignty of the written; on the other, a declaration of the impossibility

---

10. Jacques Lacan, *The Seminar of Jacques Lacan, Book XI. The Four Fundamental Concepts of Psychoanalysis*, ed. Jacques-Alain Miller, trans. Alan Sheridan, New York, Norton, 1998, p. 222.

11. Jacques Lacan, 'Conférences et entretiens dans les universités nord-américains', *Scilicet*, nos 6/7, 1975, p. 20.

of prioritizing the written oeuvre; on the one hand, refusal of sources and archives, on the other, exacerbation of the weight of the archive.

It was in order to erase this erasure of the archives, and compensate for the missing archives, that in 1990, on the advice of Olivier Bétourné, I decided to devote a book to a historical study of the genesis of Lacan's system of thought: its sources, its internal construction, and so forth. For these purposes I obviously had at my disposal his oral and written oeuvre, from which all sorts of reference-points and information could be derived. But for the purposes of recounting his intellectual career and private life, in the absence of any 'real' correspondence – a mere 250 letters – and working papers, all that was available to me were fragments of sources scattered among all those who had known the former Lacan, the childhood Lacan, Lacan before Lacan, whose archives were available.

And it is because such archival research had never been undertaken that my book on Lacan ended up being received as a biography, when the word biography does not feature in it. At all events, it is the source on which other books now draw, as if, without intending to, I had become the sole holder of a non-deposited archive.

While it is possible to write several histories of Lacan's thought, there is only one sketch of his life prior to his becoming a public figure. Indeed, we know virtually nothing about Lacan's childhood, of which I have been able to gather the only possible trace through oral testimony – that of his brother Marc-François, with whom I kept up a long, still-unpublished correspondence; and that of his sister, whom I questioned many times. But we shall never know much about this period of his life, because the archives are non-existent and the witnesses are dead.

8

SPEECH, VOICE

For twenty-six years (1953–79) Lacan talked constantly, nearly every week – Wednesday lunchtime – in a seminar that forms the bulk of his teaching. And his voice served as a reference-point for his followers. Like a cantata, his speech thrilled several generations of listeners. Three Parisian locations: the Saint-Anne Hospital (1953–63), the École normale supérieure (1964–68), and the law faculty of the Panthéon (1969–79). Three moments: the still private moment of the development of a clinical practice; the more extensive one of his entry into the intellectual field; and finally the moment of his apotheosis, immediately followed by twilight.

As we know, speech plays a leading role in the history of psychic therapies: it treats, mends, makes it possible to lift curses, and is sometimes the equivalent of a confession. It possesses cathartic powers akin to the drama of the Greek tragedians, whose heir Freud liked to think himself. It allows the patient to detach herself from her illusory pretention to self-mastery and the therapist to come up with new, liberating interpretations.

Claude Lévi-Strauss readily compared psychoanalytic therapy to shamanistic healing methods. In the one, he stressed in 1949, the sorcerer speaks and prompts abre-action – the liberation of the sick person's emotions – while in the other this role falls to the doctor, who listens in a relationship where it is the sick person who speaks. Over and above this comparison, Lévi-Strauss showed that in western societies 'psychoanalytic mythol-ogy' also served as a system of collective interpretation: 'A considerable danger thus arises: The treatment . . . far from leading to the resolution of a specific disturbance within its own context, is reduced to the reorganization of the patient's universe in terms of psychoanalytic interpretations.'[12]

If, when perverted, psychoanalysis can become an instrument of domination that does not speak its name, speech can also be transformed into a tool of destruc-tion when it serves as a medium for anathemas, rumours and conspiracies. When manipulated by dictators or gurus who know how to harness peoples' hatred to direct it against elites, it becomes odious, deceptive, vicious. As is well known, Hitler's speech and voice perverted the German language while exercising a power of hypnotic fascination over crowds.

---

12. Claude Lévi-Strauss, 'The Sorcerer and His Magic', in *Structural Anthropology*, trans. Claire Jacobson and Brooke Grundfest Schoepf, Harmondsworth, Penguin, 1977, p. 183.

Possessed of a veritable passion for orality, Lacan spoke in a voice that was soft, booming or syncopated: a mixture of Sacha Guitry for the old France side of things and of Salvador Dali for the sense of modernity. He declaimed as he ate, devouring his favourite foods – truffles, asparagus, ortolans – and beings and things alike. And that is why he turned the human voice into a powerful object of desire and seduction, while stressing that it was the vehicle of language, conceived as a system located inside linguistic phenomena. Drawing on the name of André Lalande, author of a famous *Vocabulaire technique et critique de la philosophie*, he coined a neologism – '*lalangue*' – to define the articulation of desire with the language system, or a form of knowledge that knows itself unbeknownst to itself and eludes mathematization – that is, control, formalization and full, rational transmission.

Lacan manufactured dozens of words to refer to acts of language, the language system and speech: *apparoler, bafouille-à-je, lalanglaise, langager, langagien, lituraterre mi-dire, métalanguer, par-dit, parlêtre, parlance*, and so forth.

Lacan yelled and made noises, some of them scarcely human. Lacan cajoled, caressed, seduced, shouted. Lacan imitated the cries and whistles of animals, as if to remind himself of the Darwinian origin of the totemic meal: '*père Orang*', he said. Guttural noises, chuckles, ruminations: he let his body speak as much in its silences as in a gasp accompanying some histrionic gesticulation. Lacan was theatrical, ludic, similar to Charcot's hysterics, always inclined to invent the most exuberant figures of discourse: 'I think of what I am where I do not think to think.'

In 1972, dressed in an extravagant flowing shirt, Lacan gave a filmed lecture at Louvain University. Confronted with a situationist student who spattered his lectern with milk, he reacted in a disillusioned tone, responding to the mess and the rebellious gesture with a kind of indifference. And then, all of a sudden, seized with anger, in a tone of outrage he launched a terrifying diatribe at his audience: 'Death belongs to the domain of faith . . . You are quite right to believe that you are going to die, obviously . . . it sustains you. If you didn't believe that, how could you bear your life?'[13]

If Deleuze was a Socratic master whose voice seemed to be carried by a Charles Trenet song, and if Derrida translated written texts into spoken words, punctuating them with hand gestures, Lacan improvised even when he gave the impression of reading an already written lecture: elusive archive. He passed from confidentiality to elation while sprinkling his talk with wordplay, calculated slips, or mocking remarks.

Lacan was always dazzled by a thing and its opposite: prohibition and transgression, the family and its internal

---

13. In Élisabeth Kapnist's film, *Jacques Lacan, la psychanalyse réinventée* (2001). I have used this archival material, which contrasts with Benoît Jacquot's film documentaries *Jacques Lacan: la psychanalys 1* and *2*, where we see Lacan traditionally dressed and replying in a composed voice to the questions of an invisible interlocutor. On Lacan's voice, readers are referred Claude Jaeglé's beautiful book, *Portrait silencieux de Jacques Lacan*, Paris, PUF, 2010. Cf. also the same author's *Portrait oratoire de Gilles Deleuze aux yeux jaunes*, Paris, PUF, 2005.

depravities, the symbolic order (language, signifier, reason) and the irrupting real (the heterogeneous, the accursed share, insanity), and, finally, by imaginary capture (the mirror) and its destitution (the deposed object).

He constantly rotated the three elements of his topography: the imaginary, the symbolic and the real.

Seduced by torsions, he invented the matheme, modelled on the mytheme, to refer to an algebraic script capable of accounting for the concepts and discourse of psychoanalysis. At the same time, he advanced the idea that it was necessary to break the order of conceptuality by subjecting it to subversion – that of the Borromean knot – which would undo the primacy of the symbolic over the real and the imaginary. On the one hand, a model of language articulated with a logic of the symbolic order; on the other, a model of structure based on topology and effecting a radical displacement of the symbolic towards the real, of order towards disorder.

Familiar to all specialists in topology, the coat of arms of the Milanese Borromeo dynasty comprised three rings in the form of a trefoil, symbolizing a triple alliance. If one of the rings is removed, the three are free and each refers to the power of one of the family's three branches. Thus, in his own way, Lacan perpetuated the Greek mythology that was so precious to Freud and so present in his own destiny – on condition, however, that it is constantly reinvented so as never to have any connection with a history of vinegar merchants.

9

FRAGMENTS OF A SEMINAR

Spoken, transcribed, reconstructed or recorded, for a quarter of a century Lacan's seminar was the site where the battles of Freudianism unfolded and the laboratory of a form of thought which, with its reference to Baroque art, seemed intent on imitating Francesco Borromini's trompe l'oeil façades. But it was also the site of a kind of long-running banquet where, via the magic of a voice, the sounds and images of History's great theatre, with its dramas and convulsions, were exhibited. The extent to which, throughout his life, Lacan remained a sensual spectator of the turmoil of the world, and a lucid commentator on the politics of nations, cannot be overstated. Nor did he hesitate to express his jealousy or distrust. He could be hateful and contemptuous. He left none of his listeners indifferent.

It was between 1953 and 1963 that he developed
the basics of his intellectual system. Surrounded by
excellent followers – Serge Leclaire, Wladimir Granoff,
Maud Mannoni and Jean-Bertrand Pontalis were
unquestionably the most brilliant of them – and
supported by a remarkable generation in search of new
inspiration, for ten years he offered the best of himself
to those around him. Thus the seminars of this period,
when Lacan had his followers intervene, carry traces of
that golden age of a free-ranging psychoanalysis which
dreamed of changing the fate of humanity: *The Object
Relation*, *The Formations of the Unconscious*, *Desire
and its Interpretation*, *The Ethics of Psychoanalysis*,
Transference, *The Four Fundamental Concepts of
Psychoanalysis*, and so on.

At the point when Lacan engaged in his vast
commentary on Freud's oeuvre he had just accomplished his recasting of psychoanalytical doctrine by
drawing on Saussurean linguistics, Roman Jakobson's
theses, Claude Lévi-Strauss's analysis of myths and,
finally, Heideggerian philosophy. 'Return to Freud'
was his term for this structuralist sublation whereby
he sought to extricate the Viennese theory from its
biological model. In 1957, in particular, with his seminar on *The Formations of the Unconscious*[1] – one of
the most important – he claimed to re-think the functioning of the psychic apparatus on the basis of an

---

1. Jacques Lacan, *Le Séminaire. Livre V, Les Formations de
l'inconscient* (1957–58), ed. Jacques-Alain Miller, Paris, Seuil, 1998.

initial, or primary, model that possessed the structure of language.

From his first seminars, held between 1953 and 1956, Lacan made the unconscious a language, showing that men and women are inhabited by a speech which constantly prompts them to the disclosure of their being. Subsequently, he deduced from this a theory of the subject determined by the primacy of the symbolic function; and he called the element constitutive of the acts and destiny of this subject the 'signifier'. In 1955, in his magisterial commentary on Edgar Allan Poe's 'The Purloined Letter', he imparted a narrative framework to the theory.[2]

The story, set in Restoration France, is well known. The chevalier Auguste Dupin is entrusted with a task of the utmost importance. At the request of the prefect of police, he must at all costs find a certain compromising letter stolen from the Queen and hidden by the minister. Conspicuously placed between the arches of the chimney in the latter's office, the letter is visible to those who really want to see it. But the police have not spotted it, trapped as they are in the lures of psychology. Rather than noticing the obvious fact displayed before their very eyes, they attribute intentions to the thieves. For his part, Dupin requests an audience with the minister and, during the course of their

2. Jacques Lacan, 'Seminar on "The Purloined Letter"', in *Écrits*, trans. Bruce Fink, New York, Norton, 2007, Chapter 1; *The Seminar of Jacques Lacan. Book II: The Ego in Freud's Theory and in the Technique of Psychoanalysis (1954–1955)*, ed. Jacques-Alain Miller, trans. Sylvana Tomaselli, New York, Norton, 1991, pp. 191–205.

conversation, takes the object which he had noticed almost immediately.

Thus the minister is unaware that his secret has been cracked. He still believes himself master of the game and of the Queen, for to possess the letter is to hold power over its addressee: it is solely possession, not use, of the letter that yields influence. According to Lacan, no subject can be the master of the signifier and, should it think it is, it risks being trapped in the same illusion as the policemen or minister.

In 1957 Lacan progressed to another stage of his theory of the signifier by introducing the idea, borrowed from Jakobson, that Freudian displacement is akin to metonymy (sliding of the signified under the signifier) and condensation akin to metaphor (substitution of one signifier for another). On this basis, he constructed his thesis of the signifying chain: a subject is represented by a signifier for another signifier.

In his seminar on *The Formations of the Unconscious*, Lacan resumed the main elements of this theory in accordance with a ternary logic. After an introduction on Freud's *Witz*, veritable expression of a structure of the human mind, he passed on to the issue of castration from which he conjured up the incest taboo. He then turned to the dialectic of desire and want, symptom of the intermittences of the heart and love, and finished his exposition with a reflection on Christian religion and obsessional neurosis, mingling references to Melanie Klein, de Sade, Islam and the *Aufklärung* (German Enlightenment).

As ever, in these years – the most lively – he took pleasure in converting love into hate and the divine commandment ('Thou shalt love thy neighbour as thyself') into an injunction of rejection ('You are the one you hate'), as if in order to bring out in any form of relationship with the other the permanency of a negativity of the unconscious: play of light and shadow, the cruelty of the word, fantasies, projections.[3]

At the centre of this system Lacan handled the concept of the signifier in virtuoso fashion, enabling him to link the formations of the unconscious with one another: the signifier stamps the subject with a linguistic imprint by imparting meaning to dreams, jokes, lapsus and parapraxes. But it also governs the forms of desire and otherness that conform to a logic of fantasy. Finally, the signifier makes man a social and religious being, dependent on both a symbolic function and a *logos*, inherited from the old divine power.

While this system in its entirety was present in several volumes of the published *Seminar*, it was never given a coherent exposition. For Lacan's style, or rather the style of his seminar, involved digression, fugue, eroticism, wanderings. Thus, when he sought to embody his thesis on metonymy, he encouraged his audience to re-read the passage from a novel by Maupassant (*Bel-Ami*) where the hero, having eaten some oysters, slips into a dream of a universe of an

3. Jacques Lacan, *The Seminar of Jacques Lacan. Book VII: The Ethics of Psychoanalysis (1959–60)*, ed. Jacques-Alain Miller, trans. Dennis Porter, New York, Norton, 1997.

imaginary embrace, lifting the veil of words as one raises a woman's skirts. This, stressed Lacan, illuminates the essence of the metonymy of desire, that 'perpetual slippage of meaning which any discourse is compelled to hold on to'.

And just as, in Lacan, speech was always captivating, sophisticated, exalted or offensive, so for twenty-six years his seminar was for him the equivalent of a course of treatment, inducing him to think outside of himself: beyond his own limits. Clinician of speech, ear piece of the unconscious and insanity – preferably female – Lacan never knew how to engage in dialogue with anyone, other than hundreds of texts or phrases borrowed from his patients, which he incorporated into his work like so many internal voices, and with Freud – a Freud reconstructed in accordance with his desire, a Freud of whom he considered himself the sole authentic interpreter.

No one ever contemplated genuinely entering into dialogue with Lacan: 'Me, the truth, I speak', he said, knowing that the truth could never be fully stated in the absence of a dictatorship of transparency. He also claimed that it could only be half-said, like a 'half-saying', a 'half-said', or a 'noon sounded'. Without acknowledgement, Lacan referred to Igitur, Mallarmé's character, ravaged by insanity. When midnight sounds, Igitur, the last heir of his race, throws a dice and lies down in the tomb of his ancestors to realize their immemorial dream of abolishing chance and acceding to the plenitude of the Absolute, the One of the Universe, the

Book, or the abolition of meaning in favour of form. An impossible task, therefore, but one Lacan would set about at the end of his life, between the logic of the matheme and Borromean topology. In these years, Mallarmé's revolution in poetic language,[4] profoundly marked by Hegelian thought, seemed to a whole generation to be something like a twin of the Freudian revolution, of which Lacan had made himself the new interpreter.

Lacan monologued, Lacan delighted in his own speech, Lacan handled half-saying in virtuoso fashion. He loved dispensing his verbal follies to his interlocutors, blending calm and storm in them: suffocation, exhaustion, humour, incongruous gestures – all of it perfectly controlled. But Lacan knew how to listen while fooling his interlocutor. Every time I met him, I was frequently astonished by his ability to do several things at once – turn the pages of a book or take notes, seemingly without bothering about the other person – and then immediately demonstrate that he had perfectly understood what had been said to him.

In 1960, having reached the summit of a linguistic inventiveness that had not yet turned into a topological mania or an obsession with neologisms, Lacan provided a dazzling commentary on one of the most beautiful texts in the history of philosophy: Plato's *Symposium*.[5]

---

4. A great reader of Hegel's oeuvre, Mallarmé made the quest for the finitude of the Book the equivalent of absolute knowledge.

5. Jacques Lacan, *Le Séminaire. Livre VIII, Le Transfert* (1960–61), ed. Jacques-Alain Miller, Paris, Seuil, 2001.

Readers will know the theme. Around Socrates, Plato introduces six characters each of whom expresses a different conception of love. Among them are the poet Agathon, pupil of Gorgias, whose triumph is being celebrated, and Alcibiades, a politician of great beauty whose lover Socrates had declined to be, because he preferred love of the highest good and the desire for immortality – that is, philosophy. No woman is present at this banquet, where, against a background of homosexuality, all possible varieties of corporeal and intellectual love are evoked. However, it is to the speech of a mythical woman – Diotima – that Socrates defers to expound his philosophical conception of love. She is therefore the eighth character in the dialogue, which revolves around the issue of *agalma*, defined by Plato as the paradigm of an object representing the Idea of the Good.

Since antiquity, commentators on the *Symposium* had highlighted the way that Plato employed the art of dialogue to articulate different theses on love through several characters – a love always pertaining to a consciously named desire, either by each of them or by the author himself.

Lacan inverted this perspective by interpreting the unconscious desire of each character. Thus, to Socrates he allocated the role of the psychoanalyst teaching his followers a truth that eludes their consciousness. On the one hand, he stressed, therapy is based on speech; on the other, the transmission of psychoanalysis presupposes the existence of dialogue. This was a way of signifying that he was the master of a dialogue that unfolded unbeknownst to itself while being addressed to an addressee.

The idea of the Socratic banquet was already present in Freud, who readily referred to the Greek model of transmitting knowledge: a master, a disciple, a dialogue. In its early stages, his doctrine was developed within an inner circle immersed in the Viennese spirit of the early twentieth century. Convinced that the best form of democracy had been invented by the Greeks, Freud always remained a supporter of a Platonist position. In his view, the Republic of the chosen must curb murderous instincts by promoting taboos and frustration.

Lacan took up the idea by founding the École freudienne de Paris (EFP) in 1964. He adopted the word 'school', rather than 'society' or 'association', thus drawing inspiration from the Greek model. He regarded himself as a Socratic master surrounded by his best followers. And it was then that he realized that a whole generation of philosophers and literary critics was interested in his work, particularly through the teaching of Louis Althusser. Among them were Alain Badiou, Jean-Claude Milner, Henri Rey-Flaud, François Regnault, Catherine Clément, Étienne Balibar and Pierre Macherey, but also – from different horizons – Christian Jambet or Bernard Sichère. This was the context in which I was invited to join the EFP by Lacan in 1969. My mother, Jenny Aubry, had long followed him, as a result of which I had frequented him in my childhood, obviously without knowing in what his teaching consisted. And it took the publication of the *Écrits* for me to make a connection between the man and the work.

However, over the years Lacan lost sight of the conflictual essence of dialogue. Thus the banquet came to an end and the suspended letter awaiting the miracle of a future destination was forgotten.

Dazzled by edges, margins, borders, outlines, Lacan never stopped pondering the modalities of the transition from speech to writing. In an enigmatic text dated 1971, he engaged in an erudite escalation that returned him to a primordial obsession: the letter awaiting delivery.

He had returned from a trip to Japan and recounted that, flying over Siberia, he had seen furrows and river courses that resembled crossings-out. Having to speak about the relations between literature and psychoanalysis, he mentioned this episode only immediately to escape into the 'furrows' of language. And it is thus that he invented the word '*lituraterre*' to distinguish the letter from the 'littoral' (which refers to a boundary) and the 'literal' (which does not presuppose one), thus coining a new series of terms: *litura, letter, lituratterrir*.

In this account Lacan addressed Serge Leclaire and Jacques Derrida to reaffirm the idea of the primacy of the signifier over the letter. But he also commented on *The Empire of Signs*, Roland Barthes' sumptuous book on Japan, dedicated to Maurice Pinguet. In it the author described ways of living and eating, objects and places, as so many specific elements of a sign system, referring the western subject to a language whose meaning she does not understand, but whose difference from her own she grasps, like an alterity that enables her to undo the 'real' as a result of other ways of dividing up, other syntaxes: 'in a word, to descend into the untranslatable, to experience its shock without ever muffling it, until everything Occidental in us totters and the rights of the "father tongue" vacillate – that tongue which comes to us from our fathers'.[6]

Carried away by the effervescence of his own words, and the curiosity aroused in him by Barthes' book, with this 'lituraterre' Lacan seemed to be proposing a kind of return to the meaning of Lacan, a parody of the famous return to the meaning of Freud that he had previously initiated. As a result, his discourse gave it to be understood that the Japanese subject was different in Lacanian fashion from the western subject, because the letter and the signifier could be married in its language: a real without interpretation, an 'empire of signifiers' exceeding speech.

How often have I subsequently heard the master's epigones transform this unspeakable desire for the East, so essential in Lacan, into a kind of culturalism of the 'inverted other', with the 'Japanese thing' becoming for them a mirror with many follies. Lacan had always been seduced by the Far East and had learnt Chinese at the École des langues orientales. In his plunge into the heart of that language, as in his attraction to Japanese rituals, he always sought to solve the same Mallarméan mystery:

6. Roland Barthes, *Empire of Signs*, trans. Richard Howard, New York, Hill and Wang, 1983, p. 6.

how to 'write' – that is, 'formalize' – the topography of the real, the symbolic and the imaginary (RSI). '*Lituraterre*' did not solve the problem. Quite the reverse, in my view this text contributed to a sort of self-annihilation of Lacanian language:

> My critique, if it is its place to be taken for literary, could only bear, such was my effort, on what Poe makes of being a writer in forming such a message on the letter . . . Nonetheless, the ellipsis cannot be elucidated by means of some aspect of his psycho-biography; rather, this would clog it up . . . My own text would no more resolve itself by mine: the wish I might form, for example, of finally being read properly . . . To *lituraterre* myself, I shall note that I have not constructed any metaphor in the furrowing that reflects it. Writing is this furrowing itself, and when I speak of *jouissance*, I legitimately invoke what I accumulate from my audience, no less than what I deprive myself of, for this preoccupies me.[7]

Here Lacan seemed to ridicule his 'Seminar on "The Purloined Letter"'. Punctuated with sarcastic remarks and cries of anguish, his speech seemed to me at the time as rigidified as a dead letter: Igitur in the tomb.

In 1975 Jacques Derrida registered this state of affairs by broaching the issue of the purloined letter differently. He

---

7. Jacques Lacan, 'Lituraterre', in *Autres écrits*, Paris, Seuil, 2001, pp. 12–13, 18 (translation by Jack W. Stone, modified). Another version of this text figures in *Le Séminaire. Livre XVIII, D'un discours qui ne serait pas du semblant* (1971), ed. Jacques-Alain Miller, Paris, Seuil, 2007, pp. 116, 124.

stressed that a letter does not always arrive at its destination and that, in the very wording of the 'Seminar on "The Purloined Letter"', Lacan was returning to himself the indivisibility of the letter – that is, the whole: a dogma of unity.[8] Following criticisms by Foucault and Deleuze, this was the start of a fertile critique of the impasses of late Lacan, to which I was immediately sensitive and which even affected me profoundly: destination is the unpredictable, not the mastery of fate. In his way, Derrida received the work of the historian more generously than other philosophers attached to the literality of an unequivocal reading.

Anxious as ever, Lacan could not avoid examining the issue. But in order to understand his main contribution to the clinical treatment of anxiety, we must appreciate the way in which Freud introduced that notion into the field of psychoanalysis.

Concerned not to stick to traditional descriptions, Freud first of all distinguished anxiety from fear and fright. Existential in character, anxiety in his view was a psychic state abstracted from any relationship to an object: a kind of permanent expectation which, when it becomes pathological, can lead to obsessional, phobic, compulsive forms of behaviour, even to a melancholic state.

By contrast, an identifiable object is always involved in fear. One fears something that might happen: death, separation, torture, illness, suffering, physical decline, and so forth. As for fright, it is focused on an indefinable

---

8. Jacques Derrida, *The Post Card: From Socrates to Freud and Beyond*, trans. Alan Bass, Chicago, University of Chicago Press, 1987.

object. Fright is neither fear, nor anxiety. Provoked by a danger that has no object, it does not presuppose any expectation. It too can give rise to a traumatic neurosis. Freud initially argued that a being's entry into the world is the prototype of all states of anxiety. In 1924 Otto Rank took up this thesis, claiming that for the duration of its existence each subject does nothing but repeat the traumatic history of its separation from the maternal body. Whatever its audacity, this theory of primordial attachment, so fashionable today among ethologists of the human soul, presented a formidable drawback: it threatened to make childbirth and biological separation a trauma *in itself*. On this model, indeed, all neuroses are simply the consequence of a causality external to the subject: sexual abuse, war or domestic violence, illnesses, and so forth.

In 1926, responding to Rank, Freud therefore clarified his thinking in *Inhibitions, Symptoms, and Anxiety*. He distinguished anxiety about a real danger, automatic anxiety, and anxiety as signal. The first, he maintained, is caused by the danger that prompts it; the second is a reaction to a social situation; and the third is a purely psychic mechanism that reproduces a traumatic situation experienced previously, to which the ego reacts defensively.

Lacan adopted all these definitions and commented on them. But he came up with a different conception of anxiety from Freud's. In a less Darwinian and, in some respects, more ontological perspective, he made anxiety a structure constitutive of psychic organization. Thus, according to him, it is the very signifier of any human subjectivity, rather than a condition peculiar to the anxious subject, as phenomenologists believe. It arises when the lack of the object, necessary to the expression of desire, is lacking to the extent that it fastens the subject to an unnameable real that escapes and threatens it. This 'lack of the lack' suffocates desire and is then translated into fantasies of self-destruction: chaos, imaginary fusion with the maternal body, hallucinations, spectres of insects, images of dislocation or castration.

From a clinical point of view, when it becomes pathological, anxiety can be overcome if the subject manages to turn away from this traumatic real and distance itself from a dread of lack, source of disappointment. It can then grasp its signification – that is, in Lacanian terminology, refer to the big *Other*, the symbolic law that determines it in its relationship to desire.

Lacan was a master of anxiety and a past master in the clinical treatment of anxiety. Himself incapable of eluding its grasp, he considered it at once necessary to the expression of desire, impossible to elude on pain of illusion and, finally, controllable when its origin can be symbolized. Consequently – one feels like adding at a time when, together with depression, it has become the symptom of individualistic, liberal societies – it is pointless trying too hard to neutralize it with drugs. Except, obviously, when it threatens to invade subjectivity to the point of destroying it.[9]

---

9. Jacques Lacan, *Le Séminaire. Livre X, L'Angoisse* (1962–63), ed. Jacques-Alain Miller, Paris, Seuil, 2004.

10

LOVE, WOMAN

Lacan concerned himself with the relations between men and women in modern society. A libertine in his private life, he could never remain faithful to a woman, but never wanted to leave one, concealing from one what he was up to with another. Did he experience the decidedly Freudian fear of suffering from a new separation each time? Love in the romantic sense was alien to him and love stories left him largely cold: 'Love', he said, 'is a kind of suicide'. The only thing that counted for him was the irrational, compulsive aspect of passion. From his master in psychiatry, Gaétan Gatian de Clérambault, fetishist of fabrics, and from his frequentation of madwomen and surrealist poets, he had retained the idea that love leads to the madness of *amour fou*. Also, the model of erotomania was the paradigm of his conception of love. Just as Freud was a representative of romantic love – woman, wife, mother, taboo, guilt – Lacan was the man of the dislocation of this model. He was not far from regarding love as an assault by a dark star on a persecuting object that eludes any encounter.

Seductive, anxious to please, unable to bear not being liked, he wanted to be loved, suffered from being loved and not being loved, while remaining convinced that people could not but love him – even when they hated him. A friend of women whom he admired, he addressed all of them by the formal *vous*, with hand-kissing and exaggeratedly courteous terms taken directly from the seventeenth-century literature of *préciosité*. And he had no hesitation in analysing his lovers.

But he also behaved like a temperamental child, refusing to accept that reality did not conform to his wishes. A particular kind of cigar, a particular brand of whisky, some object, certain confectionary, a certain food: everything had to be brought to him that instant, wherever he was. And in fact he nearly always managed to persuade his host to yield to his requirements. Any argument would do: okay, if you have no asparagus, give me truffles, and if you have no truffles, give me ortolans or tea – Japanese, preferably – with this make of chocolate. And if you cannot find them round here, have them sent by express delivery. An implacable, unforgettably amusing logic.

Lacan had his letters taken to the dwelling of his addressee to ensure that they reached him or her. Out of snobbery, he enjoyed dropping the names of famous people in conversation. Similarly, as if in order to avenge his origins, he loved frequenting the great and the good: thinkers, stars, journalists, actors, politicians, writers.

Françoise Dolto, whom he addressed with the informal *tu* and occasionally treated as a 'tough one', was his greatest friend. Without him, she would probably not have had the same clinical career; and without her, he would not have been what he was. For decades they formed an atypical couple, without however practising therapy in the same way: 'You do not need to understand what I say', he remarked, 'because, without theorizing, you say the same thing as me.' She asked why he never spoke of his early childhood, why he was so anxious about his image, so bothered about his appearance. Why did he need to wear such luxuriant clothes and frequent masked balls? In her letters she addressed him like the children in her consulting room, not in order to infantilize him, but to restore to the unduly infantile adult he had become the childhood of which he had been deprived. All her life, she tried to reconcile him to the idea that a mother can be something other than an ogre and a father more than an inadequate figure.

Lacan was always concerned to contrast the discourse of the unconscious – that of *jouissance* and repetition in the raw state – with the discourse of courtship rituals, of love – and hence semblance, so necessary to the amorous relationship. In love, he said, one loves oneself; the mirror is empty; the one whom I love is not the one I think I perceive. Contrary to a certain phallocentric tradition of psychoanalysis, Lacan strove to demonstrate that in love the two partners are in no wise complementary: the man exhibits his impotence, the woman her uncertainty. To define modern man, severed from his original virility, he coined numerous terms: *hommoinzin*, *hommelle*, *hommelette*, *hommodit*.

Lacan was impolite, amusing, offensive, insatiable.

An accomplished reader of certain texts, he regarded stupidity as a perversion. During a TV broadcast, 'La marche du siècle', where I found myself alongside Françoise Giroud, Catherine Deneuve and a few psychoanalysts, I was violently attacked by a journalist who also persisted in abusing Lacan, Freud, psychoanalysis, clinical and academic psychologists, psychiatrists, and especially the psychological-support units set up after major accidents. I was accustomed to this kind of aggression, but that evening I was unable to respond. Then Jean-Marie Cavada turned towards Françoise who, in her inimitable style, let loose this sentence of Lacan's: 'There's a lot psychoanalysis can do, but it's powerless against stupidity.' Therewith she put a stop to the flood of words.[1]

According to Lacan, man is the slave of semblance,[2] compelled, in order to exist, to flaunt a vigour he does

---

1. 'La marche du siècle', 19 March 1997.
2. Jacques Lacan, *Le Séminaire. Livre XVIII, D'un discours qui ne serait pas du semblant* (1971), ed. Jacques-Alain Miller, Paris, Seuil, 2007.

not control, whereas woman is closer to a truth test – a kind of writing or 'archi-writing' that enables her to elude semblance. In addition, woman is 'not-all', a 'supplement', while man needs to be an 'at least one' – a 'whole', or, failing that, a semblance of the Whole. Hence the aphorism: 'There is no sexual relationship'[3] – which means that the amorous relation is not a relationship, but a struggle between two opposites, each in an asymmetrical position vis-à-vis the other. Love compensates for this lack of sexual relationship: 'Love is giving what you don't have to someone who doesn't want it'; or, 'I ask you to refuse what I offer because it isn't that.' Lacan designated love (*amour*) in different ways, in between soul (*âme*) and dying (*mourir*): *l'a(mur)*, *amourir*, *amort*, *âmer*.

As for Freud, like many Viennese he was fascinated by human sexuality. He thought that a girl wanted to be a boy and that, as she grew up, she aspired to be the mother of a child conceived by her own father. Thus she had to detach herself from her mother – her first love – to attach herself to an object of the other sex, a substitute for the father. Freud was a firm believer in the aberrant idea that girls are haunted by 'penis envy' – a thesis that was to be refuted by his English followers, notably Melanie Klein.

While being the supporter of a sexual monism – libido

---

3. Jacques Lacan, 'L'étourdit' (1973), in *Autres écrits*, Paris, Seuil, 2001, pp. 449–97. The two most interesting commentaries on this text are by Jean-Claude Milner, *L'Oeuvre claire*, Paris, Seuil, 1995, and Alain Badiou and Barbara Cassin, *Il n'y a pas de rapport sexuel*, Paris, Fayard, 2010.

is the same for both sexes – Freud regarded any argument based on the supposedly natural instinct of sexuality as erroneous. In his view, there was no such thing as a 'maternal instinct' or female 'race', other than in the fantasies and myths constructed by men and women. As for sexual difference, he reduced it to an opposition between a separating *logos* – the male principle symbolized – and a prolific 'archaicness', a kind of maternal disorder prior to reason. Hence his famous formula: 'anatomy is destiny'.[4]

Yet Freud never argued that anatomy was the only possible destiny for the human condition. Evidence of this is the fact that he borrowed the sentence from Napoleon, who sought to inscribe the future history of peoples in politics, rather than a constant reference to old myths.[5]

With this formula, Freud reasserted the value of the tragedies of antiquity for staging the great issue of sexual difference via a political dramaturgy. Henceforth, with him and after him, and as a result of the deconstruction of the western family – background to the emergence of psychoanalysis – men and women were supposedly condemned to an idealization or debasement of one another, without ever achieving a genuine wholeness.

---

4. Cf. Sigmund Freud, 'On the Universal Tendency to Debasement in the Sphere of Love' (1912), in *On Sexuality*, Pelican Freud Library Volume 7, ed. Angela Richards, trans. James Strachey, Harmondsworth, Penguin, 1977, p. 259.

5. During a meeting with Goethe in Erfurt on 2 October 1808, the Emperor referred to the tragedies of fate which, according to him, belonged to a darker age: 'What does fate matter to us today?', he remarked, 'Politics is destiny.'

The sexual scene described by Freud drew inspiration from the world stage and war between peoples conceived by the Emperor, while prefiguring a new war of the sexes, at stake in which would one day be the reproductive organs, in order to introduce the language of desire and *jouissance* into it.

If anatomy is intrinsic to human destiny for Freud, it is by no means an untranscendable horizon. Such, indeed, is the basis of Freud's theory of liberty: acknowledging the existence of a destiny the better to free oneself from it.

In Lacan's perspective, woman is never the embodiment of a female essence or an anatomy. She does not exist as an invariant totality, any more than man is a master who manages to dominate her by according himself the illusion of omnipotence.

I have been able to establish that around 1948 Simone de Beauvoir sought to meet Lacan while she was writing *The Second Sex*. She telephoned him and asked his advice on how to handle the subject. Flattered, he replied that it would take five or six months of interviews to disentangle things. Not wanting to devote so much time to finalizing a book that was already extensively researched, de Beauvoir suggested four meetings. Lacan refused.

Influenced by Hegelianism, de Beauvoir was bound to be interested in Lacan's perspective. However, her references were not the same as Lacan's, since she had read the *Phenomenology of Spirit* in July 1940 and had not been influenced by Kojève's interpretation. As a result, what she retained of the notion of the mirror stage was closer to Wallon's conception than Lacan's conceptual system. And she made it the highlight of her argument: 'One is not born, but rather becomes, a woman.' Like Lacan, but by other means, the notion enabled her to leave Freud's biologism behind. Lacan had passed through Hegel and Kojève to reach Freud, whereas de Beauvoir passed through Lacan to substitute existentialism – in the Sartrean sense – for Freudian biologism. But she therewith bypassed the notion of the psyche – that is, the unconscious construction of subjectivity.

In 1958 Lacan in turn drew without acknowledgement on de Beauvoir's formula – to contradict its terms – when he revised psychoanalytical theories of female sexuality. He retained monism and the single libido (Freud), while introducing in the place of the other sex (difference) the notion of supplement, which was to enjoy success.[6] Fifteen years later, he announced that 'Woman does not exist.' Construed by British feminists – particularly, Juliet Mitchell – as a slogan that registered the scandal of the historical non-existence of women, the formula in fact betokened that any naturalization of a putative female essence was unacceptable. At all events, it was indeed a deferred response to de Beauvoir.[7]

6. Jacques Lacan, 'Guiding Remarks for a Convention on Female Sexuality', in *Écrits*, trans. Bruce Fink, New York, Norton, 2007, Chapter 27.

7. Jacques Lacan, *The Seminar of Jacques Lacan. Book XX: On Feminine Sexuality, the Limits of Love and Knowledge, 1972–1973*,

If Lacan compared femininity to a 'supplement', woman to a non-essence, love to what compensates for the lack of a sexual relationship or to what cannot be given, he introduced female sexuality into the universe of a real – or 'gaping hole' – drawing on descriptions by his friend Georges Bataille, from whom he had borrowed the idea that in every society, as in the psyche, there exists an accursed share or dark part, a remainder impossible to symbolize, something that escapes: the sacred, violence, the heterogeneous, perversion.

According to Lacan, *jouissance* is likewise a supplement that resembles neither pleasure nor satisfaction, but the quest for a lost thing – The Thing – which is unknowable for man and unspeakable for woman:[8] an orgasm that is limitless, voiceless, speechless; possession without a master; domination without dominant or dominated. Only the mystics, women more so than men, have possessed its secret – a perverse secret, as is attested by Bernini's *Ecstasy of Saint Theresa*, which so amazed Lacan. Mystics come. In the experience of their faith, they experience a *jouissance* they cannot express. God penetrates them body and soul and their ecstasy speaks in lieu of words: their convulsed faces, their swooning expressions, their dispersed members turned towards infinity.

---

trans. Bruce Fink, New York, Norton, 2000. In the French sentence 'La Femme n'existe pas', Lacan crosses out the definite article.

8. See Chapter 12, 'The Thing, the Plague'.

It is precisely because in his view woman's genitals are impossible to represent, speak and name that in 1954, on Bataille's advice, Lacan acquired Gustave Courbet's famous painting *L'Origine du monde*, done in 1866 for an Ottoman diplomat, Khalil-Bey, who lived in Paris. In it we find, in all their nudity, the open genitals of a woman just after the convulsions of love – that is, what is not shown and what is not referred to, if we set aside the discourses and sites reserved for pornography. The canvas caused a scandal and stunned both the Goncourt brothers, who deemed it beautiful 'like the flesh of a Correggio', and Maxime Du Camp, who regarded it as 'filth' fit only to illustrate the works of the Marquis de Sade. After the diplomat's death, the painting disappeared from view, passing from one private collection to another. It turned up in Budapest during the Second World War, when the Nazis seized it, and then passed into the hands of the Soviet victors, finally being resold to collectors. In the course of these travels, it had been covered with a panel of wood on which a landscape had been painted intended to conceal the eroticism, deemed too horrifying, of these genitals in the raw state.

Shocked by the sight of wide-open female genitals, which resembled those of Bataille's *Madame Edwarda* (1941), Sylvia Lacan asked her brother-in-law André Masson, husband of her sister Rose, to do a second painting to cover Courbet's. The painter created a wooden cover representing a different set of female genitals, abstract and far removed from the real ones imagined by Courbet. When we view this sketch by Masson, we have the impression that he is presenting a puritanical imitation of the original genitals, because it is a simulated representation of them. In short, a neo-painting had repressed the original work, while exhibiting it.

In 1994, after Sylvia's death, the canvas was donated to the Musée d'Orsay. Divested of its fig leaf, and free of any control, L'Origine du monde is now exposed to the eyes of all.[9]

Lacan loved to surprise visitors by carefully sliding back the panel to assert that Courbet was Lacanian *avant la lettre*: 'The phallus is in the painting', he would say, transforming a famous article by Freud on fetishism into a commentary on the canvas that masks the absence of what is intended to be concealed. I remember having seen the secret 'thing', hung in Lacan's study in La Prévôté, during a visit to Guitrancourt around 1970.[10]

There have been numerous copies of Courbet's painting by different painters, sometimes to conceal its subversive power, sometimes to proclaim it. But it was in 1989 that a feminist visual artist, Orlan, partisan of

9. Thierry Savatier has recounted the history of the painting very impressively in *L'Origine du monde. Histoire d'un tableau de Gustave Courbet*, Paris, Bartillat, 2006. In an afterword to the new edition of 2009, he advanced the hypothesis that Courbet's model was a pregnant woman. Hence the title: *L'Origine du monde*. I am grateful to him for the information he has provided, and to Georges Vigarello, who drew my attention to Orlan's performances.

10. See Chapter 13, 'Places, Books, Objects'.

perverse sex, performance art, transvestism, body surgery and revisitation of works in the western pictorial tradition, realized the most stunning Lacanian version of the painting: an erect phallus in lieu of the woman's genitals. With this 'work' entitled *The Origin of War*, Orlan sought to unmask what the painting concealed by fusing the unrepresentable 'thing' and its denegated fetish. Identifying with post-Lacanianism and gender and identity trouble – war, death, the feminine, the masculine, engendering[11] – she inverted the painter's iconography by taking Lacan's thesis on fetishism literally: 'I am a man and a woman', she declared.[12]

Such is the unexpected legacy of the politics of *jouissance* and the feminine pursued by Lacan and then adopted after his death by feminist supporters of transsexuality, whose trace we find in the current fascination (of which I have already spoken) not only with self-fiction, but also with the (generally female) exhibition of objects from the human body, or the minute description of real sexual acts, from forms of sacrificial mutilation to the most perverse practices: necrophilia and coprophilia.

How can we avoid thinking here of Charlotte Roche, the German TV presenter, and 'dominant feminist', whose book *Wetlands* was a bestseller in

---

11. See Chapter 14, 'Antigone'.
12. Orlan's 'performance' was realized before the donation of *L'Origine du monde* to the Musée d'Orsay, starting from a photographic base touched up by means of a computer programme.

2009?[13] Identified with her bodily secretions, she declares herself to be the swallower of her own shit: the other side of the 'eternal feminine', according to Lacan.

13. Charlotte Roche, *Wetlands*, trans. Tim Mohr, London, Fourth Estate, 2009. One also thinks of Eve Ensler's famous *Vagina Monologues* (1996), which enjoyed enormous success.

11

1966: THE *ÉCRITS*

In 1990, during a conference on Lacan, Jacques Derrida recalled the circumstances of their first encounter, at a famous symposium on structuralism organized in October 1966 by Johns Hopkins University in Baltimore. At the time, Lacan was afraid that the idea of collecting the quintessence of his teaching in 900 pages would end in disaster: 'You'll see', he said to Derrida, referring to the binding, 'it won't hold together'.

Such was the anxiety that racked him as soon as the issue of publication arose. '*Poubellication*' (binning/publishing), he would later say, therewith referring to the remains, residue or waste that the object of his fondest desire could become for him. '*Stécriture*' (dis-writing), he would also say in connection with his seminar, expressing with a disdainful gesture how much he affected to scorn the transition from the spoken to the written. And again: *stembrouille*, *stupidification, poubellicant, poubelliquer, p'oublier,* and so on.

Over and above his clinical practice, since 1964, with his entry into the École normale supérieure in the rue d'Ulm on Louis Althusser's initiative, and then with the creation of the École freudienne de Paris, Lacan had become a recognized, controversial thinker, like Michel Foucault, Roland Barthes, Jacques Derrida, Gilles Deleuze and others. Thus he belonged to a generation of thinkers more concerned with the unconscious structures of subjectivity than the status of the self-consciousness of the subject in its relationship with the world: thinkers more attuned to a philosophy of the concept than to existentialism.

Lacan feared plagiarism; and that is why he sought to keep his most cherished thoughts secret. In reality, however, he endlessly desired that they be recognized from one end of the planet to the other, and with the éclat they deserved. Haunted by a fear of not pleasing, he exhibited a kind of terror at the idea that his oeuvre might escape the interpretation he himself wanted to give of it. Thus he allowed the written trace of his spoken word to appear solely so as to have it circulate in the restricted milieu of Freudian institutions and journals.

He therefore preserved the typed volumes of his seminar and the off-prints of his articles, now become unobtainable, in his desk drawers, as if he never managed to detach himself from them. He looked at them lamenting – 'What am I going to do with all this?' – or distributed them by way of reward, with subtle dedications or ambiguous confidences. He exhibited them secretly, like a hidden treasure similar to the wide-open genitals of *L'Origine du monde*.

Thus did Lacan's oeuvre remain inaccessible to anyone who wished to read it normally, outside the circle of initiates. This was all the more true in that his 1932 thesis had fallen into oblivion without having been reprinted. And when, by chance, a copy turned up on the shelves of a specialist bookshop, Lacan hastened to purchase it.

It was an editor – François Wahl, with whom he had a strong counter-transferential relationship, since Wahl had been his patient – who in 1966 enabled Lacan to publish the sum of his writings, which was in fact composed of his lectures, themselves derived from his seminar.

As a result, following publication, Lacan became the author of a summa, organized by someone else, which functioned like a bible, subsequently commented on by his pupils orally. It must be appreciated that Lacan had always made an equation between his therapy and his seminar, to the extent that for his analysands attendance at the seminar was equivalent to a session: a long session, since it lasted nearly two hours; a session that was very different from the short sessions which occurred in the rue de Lille, in Lacan's consulting room.

But the magnum opus realized by Wahl also allowed Lacan to become the author of a written oeuvre different from the one formulated in his seminar, which was itself recorded and then transcribed by his pupils before being written, from 1973 onwards, by a co-author: Jacques-Alain Miller.

In this respect, the *Écrits* should be viewed less as a book than as the collection of a whole lifetime devoted to oral teaching. Hence the title *Écrits*, to signify trace, archive, something that does not come undone, does not vanish, cannot be stolen: a letter arriving at its destination. And that is why the book opens with the famous 'Seminar on "The Purloined Letter"'.[14]

This magnum opus immediately advertises its difference from the seminar, which proclaims orality: a work shared with another author. For the name of Wahl, 'obstetrician' of the texts, does not figure on the cover of *Écrits*, whereas that of the seminars' transcriber – Jacques-Alain Miller – justifiably features alongside the name of Lacan.

'I'm behind with everything I've got to do before dying and I'm finding it difficult to make progress.' This sentence, uttered in 1966 at the Baltimore symposium, encapsulates a problematic of being and time that is one of the major themes of Lacan's thinking. Hindered since childhood by his slowness and anxieties, Lacan never stopped theorizing the 'not-all' or half-saying, whereas he evinced a strong desire to master time, to read all the books he had collected, to visit all the centres of culture, to possess all objects. His legendary impatience, the

---

14. When, twenty years after Lacan's death, Jacques-Alain Miller published *Autres écrits*, he chose to place 'Lituraterre' at the head of the volume: '[this text] seemed to me to be destined to play here the role accorded in the *Écrits* to the "Seminar on 'The Purloined Letter'".' *Autres écrits*, Paris, Seuil, 2001, p. 9.

desire always to have his own way, was manifested in everyday life by various symptoms that only became more marked with age.

At the end of his life, not only did he continue to reduce the length of his sessions, to sleep fewer than five hours a night, and to drive his car without observing basic safety rules, he was also increasingly haunted by the fantasy of 'shrinking'. Dreading the marks of an old age that would put an end to his intellectual activity, he was gradually haunted by the fear of dying and seeing his words and his legacy disappear. And this led him to re-examine, back to front, the myths, words and concepts with which he had fashioned his reading of Freud's doctrine: castration, waste, genitals, *jouissance*, letter, death, mystic, trinity. Lacan thus sought to launch a perverse challenge to the literality of his oeuvre, always undone, reconstructed, or still to come.

In publishing the bulk of his written work at the age of sixty-five, he imparted ontological weight not to a mere collection of articles, but to a 'writing' defined as a founding event. This is because, thanks to Wahl, Lacan had precisely fashioned his *Écrits* as a realm of memory, subject to a subjective re-historicization: 'I thus find myself situating these texts in a future perfect ... In seeing them spread out over the years that were not very full, aren't I exposing myself to the reproach of having given into dwelling on the past [*attardement*]?'[15]

---

15. Jacques Lacan, *Écrits*, trans. Bruce Fink, New York, Norton, 2007, p. 56.

As a result, as the author of a text manufactured on the basis of other texts, derived from the spoken word, he was struck by the same symptom as his followers: he began to comment on his own written work as if it involved the work of another, anterior to himself – a big Other, God or Freud – and to make himself the spokesman of his own discursiveness. Thus it was that from around 1970 he enjoyed citing himself, referring to himself in the third person, over-interpreting his own positions, imitating his old verbal habits, '*jouljouer*', '*joycer*', '*lituraterrir*'.

Be that as it may, in the *Écrits* are to be found the various strata of the development of his thought, each of them punctuated by arresting formulas: 'The unconscious is structured like a language'; 'man's desire is the desire of the Other'; 'I, truth, speak'; 'there is no Other of the Other', and so on.

It was on 15 November 1966, after months of work and discussion, that the opus came out accompanied by a classified index of its major concepts (constructed by Jacques-Alain Miller), a critical apparatus, and a logical (as opposed to chronological) presentation of the texts. Five thousand copies were sold in a fortnight, even before any press reviews had appeared. More than 50,000 copies of the standard edition were bought and the paperback sale would beat all records for a collection of such complex texts: more than 120,000 copies for the first volume and in excess of 55,000 for the second. Thereafter, Lacan would be celebrated, attacked, hated or admired like a major thinker, and not only as an unorthodox practitioner.

Far from being an ad hoc work, *Écrits* is a summa that resembles both Saussure's *Course in General Linguistics* and Hegel's *Phenomenology of Spirit*. Consequently, it functions as the founding Book of an intellectual system which, depending on the era, can be read, criticized, glossed or interpreted in many ways, the worst being that of the epigones.

12

THE THING, THE PLAGUE

A master of paradox, Lacan liked to think himself the spokesman for a veritable recasting of psychoanalytical doctrine, which I have termed an orthodox sublation of Freudianism. Sublation – *Aufhebung* in German – because it involved a revolutionary gesture; orthodox, because Lacan claimed to find in Freud's text, in what he called 'The Thing', the essence of this renovation: 'At the same time return signifies a renewal starting from the foundations'; 'the meaning of a return to Freud is a return to the meaning of Freud'. In 1956, during the celebration of the centenary of Freud's birth, thinking against himself and his orthodoxy, Lacan even went so far as to declare that the centenary of a birth 'presupposes that the work is a continuation of the man who is its survival'.

Freud employed this noun (*das Ding*, The Thing) to refer to an irreducible kernel, an original experience, inaccessible to the subject, an unspeakable trace it could not name and in which it did not discern any object. For his successors – in particular, Melanie Klein – who were more interested in object relations than the singular relationship between subject and object, this thing resembled the archaic body of the mother, everything which modern clinicians in our depressive societies call attachment or bond, or lost attachment (or broken bond), or again, possible and impossible separation, producing (or failing to produce) 'resilience' – an overused term today.

The unnameable, then, the one found in the novels of Samuel Beckett and all the contemporary literature fascinated by abjection, filth, crime, autobiographical pathos, and direct plagiarism (without literary metamorphosis) of the life of others. 'The Thing' is the prehistoric, mute object buried in an abyss of destruction. In searching for its absent trace, people steal, ransack, reproduce a real that is more realistic than reality. They construct narratives on the basis of texts by internet users collected on the Web. A collage of things seen and said. As I have said, the whole of modern literature is infused with the perverted experience of this post-Freudian, post-Lacanian psychoanalysis: narrative transformed into sexual exhibitionism, the novel in the clutches of therapy or the presentation of cases, spectacularization of transgressive bodies,[1] pornographic language.

---

1. These themes can be found in the writings of Slavoj Žižek. Cf. Vincent Kaufmann, *La Faute à Mallarmé*, Paris, Seuil, 2011.

Lacan transformed 'The Thing' into a pure lack, a *jouissance*, through which the subject fuses with the object: paradise lost, the body reduced to its excrement, as de Sade exhibits it in *The 120 Days of Sodom* – a text in which Lacan delighted. Voice, gaze, mirror, hole, female genitals disguised as a crocodile's mouth, fragments of Joyce: such was the thing (*la chose*). Under Lacan's pen, it was subject to all sorts of metamorphoses – *achose*, *hachose*, *Achose*, *achosique* – where the privative 'a-' indicates that it is distinguished by its gap or hole, or the 'h' by its decapitation: the head severed with an axe (*hache*). Consequently, for Lacan the 'Freudian thing' was also an impenetrable secret – secret of being – whose form he took from Heidegger.

Much more so, however, the thing was the riddle, the Sphinx, the beast that kills, the truth that emerges from Freud's mouth to take 'the said beast by the horns'.[2] Once again we find the animal metaphors so dear to Lacan: something in between Max Ernst and La Fontaine.

According to Lacan, the thing (to summarize) furnished the ontological foundations of Freudian humanism – a humanism referred to as 'inhuman'. Lacan took up the critique of humanism peculiar to the whole generation of post-Auschwitz thinkers: the non-human is an integral part of humanity. For, even if he did not cite them, Lacan was familiar with Adorno's

---

2. Jacques Lacan, *Écrits*, trans. Bruce Fink, New York, Norton, 2007, p. 340.

texts, especially *Dialectic of Enlightenment*. As a result, he summoned his listeners not to a return to the essence of European soil, or to the theme of a Heideggerian forgetting of roots, but to reclamation of an era prior to nation-states – the seventeenth century, which he loved so much: the century of Baltasar Gracián or La Rochefoucauld. Ultimately, Lacan rose up against America which, he said, had betrayed Freud's message from old Europe.

And that is why, during a talk given in Vienna in 1955 very close to Freud's house, he invented the decidedly French, highly surrealist idea – one thinks of Antonin Artaud – that Freud's invention was comparable to an epidemic liable to overthrow the power of the norm, hygiene and social order: the plague. Europe against America:

> Thus Freud's comment to Jung (I have it from Jung's own mouth) – when, having been invited by Clark University, they arrived in view of New York Harbor and of the famous statue illuminating the universe, 'They don't realize we're bringing them the plague' – was turned against him as punishment for the hubris whose antiphrasis and darkness do not extinguish its turbid brilliance. To catch its author in her trap, Nemesis had merely to take him at his word. We would be justified in fearing that Nemesis added a first-class ticket home.[3]

---

3. Ibid., p. 336.

I have been able to establish that Freud never uttered this sentence and that Jung had never spoken to anyone of this story about a plague. On his arrival in the United States in 1909, with Jung and Ferenczi, Freud had simply remarked: 'They will be surprised when they know what we have to say.'

Thus, in the mid-twentieth century Lacan managed to endow a sentence with mythical value, to the point where in France everyone is convinced that Freud actually uttered it. In truth, for all Lacanians and French people these words have become the founding myth of a subversive representation of Freudian theory, which conforms perfectly to one aspect of the French exception. France is in fact the only country in the world where, via the surrealists and Lacan's teaching, Freud's doctrine has been viewed as subversive and equated with an epidemic comparable to that represented by the 1789 Revolution.

Constructed as a trompe l'oeil object, with arabesques and contortions, that sentence illustrates Lacan's conception of 'The Thing'. A secret code for initiates, it gives it to be understood that those who wish to join the circle of the renovators of Freudianism must don the armour of soldiers of the new epidemic.

Like some Aramis admirer of Fouquet, Lacan gladly addressed his listeners in the manner of a Jesuit general challenging the imperial powers. Imprecator or liberator, in his words and frenzy of knots and plaits he combined the obscurity of the German *Aufklärung* with the clarity of the French *Lumières*. And he cast Freud as a sort of Prometheus capable of defying both the Puritans of the New World and the goddess of Reason and Liberty, 'the famous statue illuminating the universe'. America, he was saying in substance, had turned Freud's doctrine into the opposite of what it really was: an ideology of happiness in the service of free enterprise, which could only be subverted by a new plague.

Unlike Freud – loyal to his Jewishness, but unfaithful to Judaism and hostile to every religion – Lacan, likewise an atheist, remained attached to the clerical institution, which he regarded as a political force, and to the idea that Christianity, and still more Catholicism, was the only genuine religion on account of its doctrine of incarnation. And he brandished it, like a European banner, against Freudian, puritan and pragmatic America.

Thus, in 1953 he wanted to persuade the pope that his theory of an unconscious submerged in language – not in the cerebral cortex – could touch the faithful without harming them.[4] In fact, convinced that religion would end up triumphing over everything, including science, he allocated psychoanalysis – a rational discipline – the role of concerning itself with the real – that is, what eludes any symbolization, in short, the heterogeneous aspects of the malaise of civilization: 'The Thing', always the thing . . . The lesson is valid for our age, divided as it is between a desire for

4. He wrote a letter along these lines to his brother. I have reproduced it in my *Histoire de la psychanalyse en France*, Paris, Le Livre de Poche, 2009.

fundamentalism and an unlimited quest for *jouissance* of which contemporary literature – sexological, self-fictional and cannibalistic – is doubtless one of the principal signs.

13

PLACES, BOOKS, OBJECTS

In the history of literature, lists, inventories, episodic genealogies or catalogues have always served as a prop for creating narrative processes. Whether we think of the famous 'catalogue of ships' described at length by Homer in *The Iliad*, or the extended list made by Georges Perec in *Things*, it has to be said that there is an art of classification which fascinates masters of language.

It is as if the list, be it anarchic, ordered or deconstructed, alone possesses the power to guarantee longevity or universality to the thing named. In this respect, any list is traumatic in kind: it makes a stir. And that is probably why human beings, whatever their culture, have always had recourse to lists to attest to the fact that their history is not reducible to a hallucination or fiction. The list is thus the archival real of history, the mark of the irruption of the event, whose logic is to be reconstructed.

But lists can sometimes be salutary and sometimes fatal. If we think of lists of hostages due to be executed or, contrariwise, lists of those who can be saved from death – Schindler's list, for example – or, again, the lists in crematoria at the exit from gas chambers of the dead reduced to ashes, whose names, inscribed in a huge memorial, are the only surviving evidence of a unique existence prior to their destruction, it will be understood that the list can be something and its opposite: resistance to death and risk of death.

As regards Lacan, and in order to compensate for the lack of archives, I have kept in mine an unpublished document on which I partly relied in order to reconstruct the last years of his life: a list in the literal sense of the word. In fact, it is an inventory of the master's estate: distribution of goods between the various heirs, testimony, civil status certificates, legal statements, biographical information, and so forth.[1]

Among these texts is a full list of Lacan's property. And among this property, described in the neutral language of legal discourse – a language that nevertheless seems to gush from the gaping mouth of an ogre[2] – there is another list referring to a huge collection of objects, themselves indicated by words whose

---

1. This document runs to 300 pages of typed or handwritten pages, collected between 1981 and 1987. I cite it several times in *Jacques Lacan: An Outline of a Life and History of a System of Thought*, trans. Barbara Bray, New York, Columbia University Press, 1997. Cf. also Élisabeth Roudinesco, 'La liste de Lacan. Inventaire des choses disparues', *Revue de la BNF*, no. 14, 2003; reprinted in Éric Marty, ed., *Lacan et la littérature*, Houilles, Manucius, 2005.

2. Roland Barthes made a habit of nicknaming Lacan 'the ogre'.

referents have to be divined: a list of nouns, a verbal torrent, an avalanche of diverse terms and names that require interpretation. Such is the specification in what I would call 'Lacan's big List', in which descriptions of things and places, nomenclatures of people and objects, real or disappeared, and finally a series of events are entangled: a veritable storehouse of memory and objects.

This big List resembles the famous *Catalogue of Unfindable Objects* created by the designer Jacques Carelman, and inspired by Marcel Duchamp's montages, Lichtenberg's aphorisms, Magritte's canvasses – him again – and above all by the *Catalogue de la manufacture d'armes et cycles de Saint-Étienne*.[3] In this work Carelman lists all sorts of unusable objects, manufactured from other everyday objects, dismantled and then reassembled in accordance with a fantasy layout that endows them with the dignity of desiring machines out of a surrealist dream: a curved comb for the bald, a sleeve board shaped like a hand to iron gloves, a flat chair recommended for its small size, and so on.

A fetishistic collector, passionate about rare or original editions, over his lifetime Lacan had collected all sorts of objects – paintings by masters, water colours, designs, sculptures, archaeological figurines, valuable

3. Jacques Carelman, *A Catalogue of Unfindable Objects*, London, Frederick Muller, 1984. It is to Georg Christoph Lichtenberg (1742–99) that we owe the famous formula: 'a knife without a blade whose handle is missing'.

furniture, extravagant clothing made in accordance with
his instructions: furs, suits in unusual materials, hard
collars without flaps or collars twisted and turned up,
lavallières of various sizes, made-to-measure shoes in
rare skins, gold pieces, ingots.

Like the archives, the objects itemized in the big List
are 'unfindable'; they have been dispersed. Yet they do
not resemble Carelman's. It is via the linguistic rituals
by which Lacan's thought was captured in his last years
that we can reinterpret their meaning.

Indeed, from 1970 onwards a neologistic instinct
was blended in staggering fashion in Lacan's discourse
with an instinct for collection. For eleven years,[4] Lacan
drew from James Joyce's texts a list of manufactured
words that were like a mime of the list of things
collected. Pastiching *Finnegans Wake*, and sensing his
own mind deteriorate, Lacan deployed an art of verbal
frenzy that caused repressed family memories to emerge
from his unconscious. I am thinking of the lecture
where he referred to himself as Jules Lacue, a priest's
child; of another when he cursed the name of his grand-
father; of a third where, with *L'Origine du monde* in
mind, he referred to '*The* Mother' as a 'big crocodile in
whose mouth you are' or to Queen Victoria as a
'serrated vagina'.[5]

---

4. From 1970 until 1981.
5. Jacques Lacan, *Le Séminaire. Livre XXIII, Le Sinthome* (1975–
76), ed. Jacques-Alain Miller, Paris, Seuil, 2005. Cf. also Jacques
Aubert, ed., *Joyce avec Lacan*, with a preface by Jacques-Alain Miller,
Paris, Navarin, 1987, and Jacques Lacan, 'Joyce le symptôme', in
Autres écrits, Paris, Seuil, 2001, pp. 565–70.

Distinct from the witticism – or portmanteau word – that aims to illuminate the many facets of a language, as in Rabelais or Joyce, the neologism can turn into delirious creation if an author resorts to it to rethink the whole of a doctrinal system and, above all, to imprint his name on a discourse from which a new set of concepts can spring *ex nihilo*. In this respect, 'neologistic' excess is an abuse of language that turns thought into a pile of words, into delirium.

Lacan not only collected neologisms, objects, places, books or clothes, but also accumulated analytical sessions, as is indicated by the list of the number of patients or pupils who filed into his flat on the rue de Lille. After 1975, the duration of sessions was reduced to an absence of duration, to an absence of session.

By way of example, I shall cite the testimony of one of his analysands:

I confirm that I was analysed and supervised by Lacan at the rate of three sessions a week from 1972–76, and then six sessions from 1976–80, to which must be added one supervisory session a week from 1975. The cost of a session did not change from 1972–81 – 150 francs. The cost of a supervisory session increased from 300 to 500 francs in 1978, and the length of sessions varied, but rarely exceeded a few minutes. Whatever the time of the appointment, the two waiting rooms used by Doctor Lacan were generally full – around twelve people.[6]

6. Testimony dated 15 January 1982.

Dissolution of time, multiplication of analysands, prolif-
eration of sessions – according to some accounts, certain
people were doing ten a day, one minute every half-hour
– splitting of the sites for waiting and consulting: such is
the dissemination to be found in the big List.

While Freud arranged his Greek and Chinese figurines on his desk in order to humanize them and use
them as a support for his writing,[7] Lacan predominantly
sought to visualize objects with a *jouissance* equivalent
to what he experienced at the spectacle of the washing
of feet which he loved to attend, on the sly, in certain
Roman convents. Using objects like a mirror, he liked to
place them before guests, whose eye he sought to catch
to observe their reaction.

Lacan claimed that his taste for objects in no wise
resembled Freud's and that with him the object of collection was a 'thing beyond the object', which had no role
other than being utterly useless in itself, like Jacques
Prévert's collection of match boxes, interlocked in – or
on – one another with open or closed drawers. An accu-
mulation of remains and debris:

> For if you think about it, the match box appears to be a
> mutant form of something that has so much importance
> for us that it can occasionally take on a moral meaning;
> it is what we call a drawer. In this case, the drawer was
> liberated and no longer fixed in the rounded fullness of

7. *Berggasse 19: Sigmund Freud's Home and Offices, Vienna 1938:
The Photographs of Edmund Engelman*, introd. Peter Gay, New York,
Basic Books, 1978.

a chest, thus presenting itself with a copulatory force
that the picture drawn by Prévert's composition was
designed to make us perceive.[8]

In this relationship to the object, which served as a transition to an imaginary appropriation of the other, we
find, as ever, the mirror stage or reified object serving as
a prop for another thing. Maurice Kruk wrote in 1982
that

> In the way Lacan sometimes stated the reasons for his
> attachment to certain of the revelations afforded him
> by works of art, as a result of their power of provoca-
> tion and the reactions they made it possible to provoke
> in others, it always seemed to me that everything he
> owned was useful to him anytime for his reflection;
> that the presence of works and their customary contact
> went with his way of life. Their value stemmed either
> from bonds of family or friendship, or from the
> mysteries and enigmas they contained, which stimu-
> lated him.

When it came to books, Lacan often displayed an intense
urge to possess them at once, whereas he could have
discovered their content at the Bibliothèque nationale.
He always wanted to be the first to receive the sought-
after book duly dedicated by its author. Sometimes he

---

8. Jacques Lacan, *The Seminar of Jacques Lacan Book VII: The
Ethics of Psychoanalysis, 1959–1960*, ed. Jacques-Alain Miller, trans.
Dennis Porter, New York, Norton, 1997, p. 114.

went so far as to beg that the manuscript be sent to him, declaring himself ready to spend his last penny to be able to touch, contemplate or devour the desired thing: 'How I would like', he said to Roman Jakobson in 1951, 'to have your book on aphasia'. And he added that he knew very well that if the linguist had not sent him the work, it was because he no longer had a spare copy: 'Is it possible to find it second hand?' To acquire the object, Lacan said that he was ready to open an unlimited line of credit. Then, alluding to another book, he asked if it was the same one – that is, the one he had found refer- enced under the title *Kindersprache, Aphasie und Allegemeine Lautgesetze*, published in Uppsala in 1941.[9] That too would be precious to him, he added, if it was different from the book Jakobson had spoken to him about.

In another letter from 1958, not having managed to obtain the rare copies he had ordered in a London book- shop, Lacan asked Jakobson to send him everything he could, on condition that 'you let me pay for the expen- sive items'. And he cited *Webster's*, expressing the wish that by return mail Jakobson should present him with something which would please him.

In the numerous letters in my archives, Lacan multi- plies imprecations to demand of his correspondents that they provide him with the most valuable works without delay. And often, when he did manage to obtain them,

9. Roman Jakobson, *Child Language, Aphasia and Phonological Universals*, The Hague, Mouton, 1968. Lacan's letters derive from the Roman Jakobson collection.

he either did not return them, even though they had been borrowed, or did not pay the price agreed for the purchase, or claimed he had lost the object when the lender requested its return.

The 'thing' – book, manuscript, art work – then fell into the no man's land of a spectral absence that still haunts Lacan's heirs. As with the archives, we never know whether some particular thing has really been destroyed, lost, removed or whether, like Captain Ahab's whale, it might one day spurt out of an ocean of dusty bric-a-brac, thus entering the circuit of the pending archives. At the heart of the Lacanian saga of objects, things, books or archives, present or disappeared, no one ever knows who has what. No word, no oracle, no seer has the least sovereignty over such a realm of memory. And similarly, Lacan's big List, like the female genitals of the famous painting, resembles a continent that has been engulfed. It does not appear on any map and does not assume any designation.

The topographical inventory of Lacan's enormous memorial begins at 5, rue de Lille, with the description of the famous office and the no less famous couch of mousy grey material, which we know was sold by auction at the Drouot Hotel to an anonymous buyer on 5 October 1991.[10] The purchaser gave it to his wife, a psychologist, who found it drab and old-fashioned. He

10. The sale by auction of furniture and objects belonging to Sibylle Lacan, Lacan's second daughter from his first marriage, was conducted at her request and entrusted to Guy Loudmer. In the catalogue fifty-three items are listed, among them four lithographs by François Rouan, some old knickknacks, some rare books and a desk.

then put it in a loft, before trying unsuccessfully to re-sell it to various psychoanalysts. Will it re-emerge one day? No one knows.

Turned into a museum, the place where Lacan received his patients for forty years is thus organized around a missing object: in place of the original couch is another one – an identical replica. This museum is not comparable to the Freud Museum in London or the Freud Museum in Vienna, both of them open to the public. The former contains all Freud's objects – his collections, traces of his history and his life and that of his daughter, who lived there after his death. It is the house at 20 Maresfield Gardens, acquired by Freud during his London exile. The museum in Vienna, located at 19 Berggasse, is an empty space, pure testimony to the ghostly presence of the master prior to his exile in 1938. He lived there with his family for forty-seven years.

Unlike these two centres of Freudian memory, the Lacan Museum is a virtual, anamorphosed, unreal one. It is not visited. Only a brass plaque, fixed to the exterior of the building, indicates that Lacan did indeed live there from 1941–81.

The second major Lacanian realm of memory is La Prévôté, a country residence situated in the village of Guitrancourt and acquired in 1951. During Lacan's lifetime, it was made up of three distinct parts: the main residence; an adjoining house called the 'aquarium', 'studio' or 'library', and serving as a workroom; and, finally, a rest house located opposite the swimming pool

and constructed after 1970 on the advice of Maurice
Kruk, a Professor of Architecture whom Lacan had met
in Japan. Here Lacan had acquired the habit of indulg-
ing in the ceremony of tea. As much out of a concern for
tradition as affinity for the Far East, which he had
dreamed of from his earliest years, he had bought some
unusual old pieces – among them a bowl from the
Monoyama era jealously selected by his favourite
antique dealer.

In the big List, added to this residence, divided into
three, is the flat at 3, rue de Lille indicated as the domi-
cile of Sylvia Bataille. She lived there from October
1943,[11] surrounded by numerous paintings, books,
documents and figurines. After her death in 1993, these
objects were moved. In the List the only thing that
survives is the trace of a thousand volumes, without any
mention of their titles.

In his lifetime, Lacan moved harmoniously from one
place to the other. According to Marie-Pierre de Cossé
Brissac,

> The rue de Lille had two very clear destinations – work,
> everyday life – but you passed from one building to the
> other and the whole seemed neither huge nor illustrious.
> There was a friendly side to the meals to which I was
> invited. Sylvia – with whom he was visibly very in love
> – was in her own house like a dancer on points in the

---

11. The year in which Georges Bataille, separated from Sylvia since
1938, had separated from Denise Rollin, who then gave up the flat she
occupied at 3, rue de Lille to Sylvia.

scarcely conscious role of enchantress. Jacques manoeu-
vred things from the outset, with a thousand difficulties
and secret gibes.[12]

L'Origine du monde was not the only pictorial work
displayed at La Prévôté in the aquarium. At the heart of
the Lacanian museography figures a 'non-exhaustive'
list, a list in the big List, comprising 'western paintings',
whose theme is mainly feminine. In addition to Courbet,
we find a Monet (*Les Nymphes*), a Balthus (*Portrait*), a
Zao Wou-Ki, a Picasso (*Femme nue renversée*), a Renoir,
four works by Masson, and another by Derain (*Portrait
de Sylvia*).

Another list, internal to the big List, itemizes a
collection of Japanese prints, and another a collection
of very rare Chinese paintings: fifteen scrolls and a
dozen fans. To which is added, in the same list,
mention of another collection of various objects: a
dozen terracotta Alexandrine figurines; a dozen pieces
of pre-Columbian (Nazca) ceramics, one of which is
deemed 'exceptional'; masks and ritual objects from
South America, including a large pre-Columbian
statue; as well as fragments of Egyptian sculptures and
ivory sculptures.

In the adjoining building, where the master's office
and his 'works in progress' were to be found, were two
further spaces, described as 'rooms adjacent to the

office'. As for the second building, or 'main residence', it comprised several rooms, among them the main lounge, referred to as the 'green lounge'.

In the midst of this lay-out, formed like a labyrinth, Lacan had installed five libraries 'acquired from the Berès, Bazi, Loliée and Nicaise bookshops'. In addition to the volumes I shall refer to later, they contained an original edition of Diderot's *Encyclopédie*, another of Apollinaire's *Alcools*, fully bound in black leather, and twenty large volumes on painters entitled 'Atelier', accompanied by exceptional original engravings, modern or old – Picasso or Piranesi, for example. These are mentioned in the big List as having 'disappeared'.

It was in the office and the two adjoining rooms that Lacan's three most important libraries were assembled, the fourth being in the green lounge of the main residence and the fifth in the rooms of the flat at 5, rue de Lille. As with Courbet's painting at a later date, a sixth library was installed at 3, rue de Lille, where Lacan went every day. And it is absent from the big List, by the same token as Lacan's fifth library – the one at 5, rue de Lille. As for the library at 3, rue de Lille, the only thing attested in connection with it is the existence of a thousand volumes, to which is added mention of two cabinets of rare books, several shelves full of original editions by surrealist and classical authors, an original edition of Apollinaire's *Poète assassiné*, a complete set of the review *Le Minotaure* and, finally, some manuscripts by Georges Bataille.

Let us now come to the twenty-eight pages of the document that itemizes the books in the only one of Lacan's libraries of which we possess a written trace: the large library at La Prévôté. Distributed over two sites, it is in fact made up of four libraries: one situated in the main residence and the other three in the detached house and adjoining rooms. This large library, of which only the list is known, was assigned during the division of Lacan's possessions to one of the sons of his eldest daughter,[13] who, in order to shield it from prying eyes, had a pavilion built in the heart of the countryside, fitted out in accordance with the most sophisticated security standards. It comprises 5,147 volumes.

Since these books are invisible, it is impossible to know with any degree of certainty which of them had been read by the master, which passages he possibly underlined, and what his references were when he cited a work approximately in his seminar. And, as his oral oeuvre has been edited without bibliographical notes or contextual references, the causal link between its elaboration and the books accumulated by Lacan during his lifetime is condemned to gradual dissolution. This situation has led the various transcribers of the seminars, and indexers, to engage in an escalation of interpretation which becomes excessive.[14]

---

13. Fabrice Roger-Lacan, son of Caroline Lacan (1937–73), from Lacan's first marriage.
14. The totality is available on the internet.

The list of books in the large library only itemizes classical works in the western and eastern traditions:[15] *One Thousand and One Nights*, Ibn Khaldun, Goethe, Cervantes, Dostoevsky, Larbaud, Shakespeare, all the major Russian authors, all the great British novelists, dozens of books of art or devoted to the history of art, Leconte de Lisle, Homer, Sophocles, Cicero, Herodotus, Caesar, Tallemant des Réaux, Ariosto, Scarron, Huysmans, de Sade (in several editions), Casanova's *Memoirs*, Courteline, Baudelaire, Nietzsche, an avalanche of scientific works (Lagrange, Renouvier, Cournot, Cuvier, Cabanis, Bichat, Duchenne de Boulogne, etc.), Rimbaud, Léon Bloy, Malthus, Proudhon, Marx and Engels (forty-two volumes), Hegel, Blanqui, Smith, Kautsky, Novalis, Fourier, Lassalle, Louis Blanc, Marat, Lenin, Bakunin, Rivarol, the original texts from the Damiens trial, Descartes, Fénelon, Barrès, Brissot, Lamennais, dozens of books on medicine, the thirty-eight volumes of the complete works of Balzac, a whole panel of German writers, histories of Chinese civilization, Mexico, the Talmud, Kant, Maine de Biran, Saint-Simon, Gracián, Saint-Beuve, Germaine de Staël, André Chénier, Rousseau, Chateaubriand, d'Holbach, Malebranche, the Garnier classics (thirty-four volumes), the 'La Pléiade' collection containing several albums (twenty-six volumes), Michelet, Théophile Gauthier, Taine, Mérimée, Eugène Sue, Nerval, the Dreyfus affair, Plato, the Bible (Sacry's

---

15. I cite the titles in the order in which they appear on the list.

translation), Rimbaud, Cendrars, Apollinaire, Diderot, Racine, Ronsard, Montaigne, the complete plays of the Latins, Catulle Mendès, Benjamin Constant, Bonald, Auguste Comte, Quinet, Cabet, Flora Tristan, Mably, thirty-four volumes of metaphysics, twenty-three volumes of Aristotle, sixty volumes of mathematics and geometry, Boccaccio, and Kierkegaard.

Added to this set of classics is another, made up of twentieth-century authors: Gide (twenty-eight volumes), Havelock Ellis (twelve volumes of *Études de psychologie*), Henry Corbin, Breton (collection of sculptures and neo-Caledonian documents), accompanied by all sorts of works (fifteen volumes) on the Kanak, Easter Island, the Papous, and so on, as well as forty-seven softback or bound volumes on Oceania and Central America; thirty-three volumes of psychology and philosophy, nine volumes from congresses of psychiatry, forty-five volumes by Jung, Malinowski and others, and twenty-two volumes by Aragon (with his signature), some of them first editions; Einstein, Poincaré, Curie; Bonnefoy, Saint-Pol-Roux, Dos Passos, Hemingway, Camus, Fargues, Vaillant, Mandiargues, Crevel, Max Jacob, a complete set of *Temps modernes*, Bachelard, Claudel, Althusser, Malraux, Dumézil, Claudel, Paulhan, Todorov, Paul Zumthor, Marc Oraison, Jérôme Peignot, Maria-Antonietta Macciocchi, Maurice Rheims, Proust (fifty volumes), Artaud's *Le Pèse-nerfs* in a first edition, eighty-eight volumes of Freud in German, English and French, fifty volumes of psychiatry, thirty-four volumes and assorted pamphlets on psychoanalysis, thirty-nine volumes of the *International Journal of Psychoanalysis*, four volumes of the *Zentralblatt*,[16] Sartre, Merleau-Ponty, Jean Wahl (fifty volumes), Butor, Mishima, Leiris, Michaux, Bataille, Éluard, Duras, Ponge, Bousquet, Joyce, Caillois, thirty-five volumes of Heidegger and other German philosophers, thirty-one volumes in English, and twenty-three volumes on the unconscious and psychoanalysis.

The main list lacks an inventory of works by analysands, fellow analysts and pupils: letters, books, accounts. What happened to them? Where are Marguerite Anzieu's manuscripts?

For over thirty years, followers, pupils, patients and authors, famous or unknown, sent, brought or deposited with Lacan – sometimes entrusting them to his secretary – their works, with a dedication. Some people gave him manuscripts, translations, private diaries, various objects, documents, paintings, archives – all of them things that do not feature either in the big List or in any other list or sub-list. Lost, mislaid, forgotten, repressed, these things seem never to have arrived at their destination, as if the time for understanding had already passed together with the time for concluding: a highly Lacanian parable.[17]

---

16. *Zentralblatt für Psychanalyse. Medizinische Monatschrift für Seelenkunde.* Founded by Freud in 1910, this journal ceased publication in 1912. *International Journal of Psychoanalysis (IJP)*: journal founded by Ernest Jones in 1920, which subsequently became the official organ of the IPA.

17. Cf. Jacques Lacan, 'Logical Time and the Assertion of Anticipated

For all those who offered Lacan a fragment of themselves might imagine that these marks of themselves exist somewhere – stored in a loft, a cupboard, a cellar, a chest. However, like children born out of the blue, they might also think that these things never existed, since no response has ever been given to their search for a trace of their past.

Wherever they are, these things are now chimeras. And, as regards such a distressing situation, thirty years after his death Lacan's big List has become the only archival evidence confirming that objects, books, things, documents, whole lives spoken and recounted, did indeed exist, while others have disappeared or become unfindable.

Not once in the big List do we ever come across the least mention of the names of Lacan's principal followers: no list of their works, their letters, or any kind of exchange. Yet I know, through their testimony, that between 1970 and 1980 they regularly sent the master their books, articles, off-prints, pamphlets and numerous letters.[18]

Consequently, it is as if, under the words of the big List, the shadow of another list is outlined: the list of texts and people who have disappeared. A veritable cartography of all the objects awaiting delivery, this other list, obscure and diffuse, peoples the imaginary of those who have been dispossessed of their privacy and

---

Certainty', in *Écrits*, trans. Bruce Fink, New York, Norton, 2007, Chapter 9.

18. I have collected around fifty convergent testimonies.

who, through Lacan's oeuvre, itself disseminated, wish to be the inheritors of a potential preservation of the master's memory.

Perhaps there is a connection between the Lacanian ritual of collection – of which at present we possess only the big List – and what I have called the 'laboratory of the extreme'[19] constituted by the experience of therapy in Lacan's last years. An experience that referred each analysand to the existential nothingness of a broken temporality: that of the session reduced to an instant. Vainly seeking for a hypothetical logical formalization of psychosis, Lacan had transformed the analytical session into an epiphany that simulated the moment of death. And consequently, caught in a maelstrom of constant levitations, all the subjects engaged in sessions believed they were able to inherit a meaningful interpretation in a fraction of a second, whereas they were captured by the frenzy of the neologism. Instead of speech, everyone received its formula, its seal, its mark, its letter.

And it is thus that, in the list of Lacan's neologisms – which strangely repeats the big List of disappeared things – everyone continues to search for a feature with which to identify. And perhaps, carried along by the mystique of this latter-day language, they will one day seek to create as many schools, journals, collections, opuscules or groupuscules as Lacan manufactured

19. Cf. Élisabeth Roudinesco, *Jacques Lacan: An Outline of a Life and History of a System of Thought*, trans. Barbara Bray, New York, Columbia University Press, 1997.

neologisms. A thousand variants might then serve to amplify the list of 'lacano-contemporary' discourses to infinity: that of *lalangue, parlêtre, sinthome, lituraterre, unebevue*; but also *jaclacque, stécriture, poubellication* or *hainamoration*. That would represent the twilight of Lacanianism.

Yet even if the big List, whose silhouette I have sketched here, is nothing but the signifier of the absence of archives, it also prompts a desire for renovation that can enable the transmission of a teaching, by dint of the fact that it stands in for the missing object.

It remains that case that, as things stand, it is as if the heirs of the master's thinking were still attached to a fixed reading of his texts, because whole sections of their history have been abolished. But we know that the only way of keeping a conceptual and clinical legacy alive is to be unfaithful to it.

Such is doubtless the lesson to be drawn from what remains to us of Lacan, as of his commentary on 'The Purloined Letter', read back to front: no one is the master of fate, not even the fate that forever takes byways.

14

ANTIGONE

Everyone knows the story of the family of the Labdacids, taken up by Sophocles in his famous trilogy
Oedipus Rex, *Oedipus at Colonus*, and *Antigone*.[1] To
avert the fulfilment of the Oracle of Apollo, which has
predicted that he will be killed by his son, Laius,
husband of Jocasta, hands his new-born son over to a
servant after first having his feet pierced. Rather than
taking him to Mount Cithaeron, the latter entrusts
the boy to a shepherd who gives him to Polybius, the
childless King of Corinth. Having reached adulthood,
Oedipus, thinking to escape the prophecy, sets out for
Thebes. On the way he encounters Laius and kills him
in the course of a brawl. He solves the riddle of the
Sphinx and then marries Jocasta, whom he neither

---

1. Third in chronological order, *Antigone* was the first play in the
trilogy composed by Sophocles (442 BC).

loves nor desires, and with whom he has four children: Antigone, Ismene, Eteocles and Polyneices. When the plague descends on the city, he seeks to discover the truth which Tiresias, the blind seer, knows. A messenger, the old servant, announces the death of Polybius, but also tells Oedipus how he received him from the hands of the shepherd. Jocasta hangs herself, Oedipus blinds himself, and decides to end his days in exile with Antigone at Colonus, under the protection of Theseus.

It is then that his two sons, cursed by their father, dispute his succession and end up by killing one another. One – Eteocles – remains faithful to Creon, brother of Jocasta and the new King of Thebes, while the other – Polyneices – rebels. Violating the laws of the city and hospitality, Creon refuses him any burial. Antigone sets herself against Creon and he condemns her to an atrocious death. She will be shut up between two walls in an underground room: 'It is your spirit of independence that has doomed you', says Creon, whose son Haemon, in love with Antigone, accompanies her into her tomb. When she hangs herself, as had Jocasta, he stabs himself to death. Likewise cursed by the gods for having dishonoured a dead person, Creon will see his work ruined and his family destroyed. For the laws of the city must be in harmony with those of the gods.

For the Greeks, Oedipus is a tragic hero flawed by excess. He believes himself powerful on account of his knowledge and wisdom, but is compelled to discover

that he is other than what he thinks he is: a stain that
disturbs the order of generations, a 'lame man', son and
husband of his mother, father and brother of his children, killer of his father.

When Freud seized on this story in 1896, he redi-
rected the Greek meaning of the tragedy, making
Oedipus a hero guilty of unconsciously desiring his
mother to the point of wanting to kill his father, thus
linking psychoanalysis to the fate of the modern bourgeois family: deposition of the father by the son and
aspiration to fusion with the mother as the original
figure of all emotional attachments. And, without
concerning himself with his exile, Antigone or Creon,
he linked the fate of Oedipus – figure of the unconscious – to that of the Christian prince Hamlet,
embodiment of the guilty conscience. For Hamlet is
unable to rise to the challenge issued by his father's
ghost: to kill the tyrant Claudius, the usurper who has
married his mother.

If Freud had the stroke of genius, not to invent the
Oedipus complex, but to transform every subject of
bourgeois modernity into a tragic hero, it has to be
said that all renovators of his doctrine have been
compelled to reactivate the heroic dynasties that
presided over the birth of psychoanalysis. For this
discipline is not a science, but rather a rational statement whose background is great myths constantly
reinterpreted in accordance with the history of the
world: it is a philosophical anthropology of the human
condition.

Melanie Klein became attached to Orestes and the family of the Atreides, while many others inclined to Narcissus. Lacan was no exception. And it is no accident if he dropped *Oedipus Rex* and primarily concerned himself with the blind old man exiled at Colonus and then with Antigone, his accursed daughter.[2]

Like many other French thinkers in the second half of the twentieth century – Sartre, Derrida, Foucault, Lyotard, de Beauvoir, Deleuze – Lacan, as we have said, inscribed the caesura of Auschwitz as a founding element in any renewal of psychoanalysis. And this was the perspective, extending his reflection on the western family, from which he engaged in a magisterial interpretation of Sophocles' two tragedies between 1954 and 1960.[3] For Oedipus King of Thebes and tyrant of excess, he substituted Oedipus at Colonus, the blind old man detached from his sovereignty and stripped of the attributes of paternity.

After the Second World War, the extermination of the Jews had come to signify to humanity the extent to which the idea of the destruction of the *genos*, peculiar to the story of the Labdacids, could be inscribed at the

---

2. Jacques Lacan, 'Desire, Life and Death', in *The Seminar of Jacques Lacan, Book II: The Ego in Freud's Theory and in the Technique of Psychoanalysis, 1954–1955*, ed. Jacques-Alain Miller, trans. Sylvana Tomaselli, New York, Norton, 1991, pp. 221–34; 'The Essence of Tragedy', in *The Seminar of Jacques Lacan, Book VII: The Ethics of Psychoanalysis*, ed. Jacques-Alain Miller, trans. Dennis Porter, New York, Norton, 1997, pp. 243–90. On Hamlet, cf. *Le Séminaire. Livre VI. Le désir et son interprétation* (1958–59), unpublished, and Roudinesco, *Jacques Lacan: An Outline of a Life and History of a System of Thought*.

3. It was to be praised by Pierre Vidal-Naquet.

heart of the unique genealogy of each subject. And as a result, confronted with an era of catastrophes, the practice of psychoanalysis could not dispense with reference to this major instance of man's annihilation by man. Freud had obviously sensed this in expounding his theory of the death instinct and selecting the cursed family of the Labdacids to illustrate the fate of modern subjectivity. That is why Lacan, breaking with the Oedipal bonhomie of the revolt of sons against fathers,[4] and forging ahead with his conception of the female 'supplement', would choose as the emblem of his renovation a woman – Antigone – who assumed her martyrdom as an absolute, to the point of rendering her killer (Creon) more 'human' than his victim by dint of his very baseness.

In Lacan's view, Antigone embodies a deadly trajectory 'between two deaths'. Between the moment when, for having sought to prevent her brother dying a second death without a burial, she is walled up in a cave, and the moment when she hangs herself, she endures a dreadful ordeal. Cancelled from the world of the living without yet being dead, she is thereby reduced to a 'between-two-deaths'. Here Lacan draws equally on a Christian tradition – that of the transition from death to hell – and on a remark by de Sade, who dreamed of committing a crime that would be followed by the effacement of the crime and

4. 'The Oedipus complex', he correctly said, 'is Sophocles' little story minus the tragedy.'

the disappearance of any trace of the body. Hence annihilation: a murder followed by a double disappearance – of the bodies and of the traces of the criminal act.

Far from being a 'cannibalistic' rebel challenging authority – morning twilight or unhappy consciousness – as an interpretative tradition from Hölderlin via Hegel to Heidegger would have it,[5] Lacan's Antigone bore the burden of one death leading to another death. Designated as a soul whose intolerable brilliance was the sign of a deadly inheritance, she was referred to a maternal genealogy (Jocasta), source of all disorders. What is fascinating about her, said Lacan, is that she takes on the essence of the genocidal drive because she sacrifices the future to the past by asserting that a brother is more irreplaceable in the family than a child or husband. Such is Antigone's 'inhumanity' – non-negotiable, inflexible, beyond fear and pity.

Once more, Lacan became attached to the image of a young madwoman draped in her 'virginal difference', neither woman nor mother, refusing the love of her lover – who commits suicide with her – as well as procreation: 'We see the child Antigone: she groans, screaming like the mournful bird when she sees the bed of her nest empty.'

---

5. On interpretations of Antigone and the staggering posterity of the character and Sophocles' play, readers are referred to George Steiner, *Antigones: The Antigone Myth in Western Literature, Art and Thought*, Oxford, Oxford University Press, 1986.

And by the same token, contrasting the victim's inhumanity with the executioner's humanity, Lacan regarded Creon as a kind of anti-hero, pitiful and condemned to err in the process of administering the goods of the city. And so as not to distance himself from the Freudian tradition, for which the figure of Oedipus is always associated with Hamlet, Lacan had no hesitation in comparing Shakespeare's hero with his dear Antigone. He too is 'between-two-deaths', said Lacan. Not a guilty son, but an actor in a tragedy of the impossible, the prisoner of a dead father – the ghost – and a mother who has transmitted a horror of femininity to him. It is not enough for him to kill Claudius – the first death – he must also send him to hell – second death. As a result, he does not manage to commit the requisite murder because he is too intent on futile vengeance.

Antigone, tragedy of genocide; Hamlet, tragedy of 'non-volition' and the impossible. It is not surprising that both figures reappear periodically: the first when a disaster strikes the world and the second as the truth of modern man faced with an absence of gods.

From this message, which drew an apocalyptic picture of the ghosts haunting a psyche beset by the legacy of a major crime, symbolized by the martyrdom of a woman at once rendered heroic by her act of resistance and destroyed by her intransigence, Lacan deduced that modern psychoanalysis could only construct its ethics on a principle derived from Antigone's inhumanity: not to give way on one's desire. The ethics of psychoanalysis, he was saying in substance, is not an arrangement in the service of goods (Creon), but a tragic experience of existence.[6]

In conceiving this commentary, Lacan certainly had in mind the fate of Simone Weil, a philosopher hailing from a family of the intellectual bourgeoisie, who rejected Judaism and Jewishness, and then dedicated herself to serving the proletariat, before finally moving towards Catholic faith without ever converting: between two stories, between two deaths. Having joined the Gaullist Resistance, she let herself die at the age of thirty-four in a sacrificial gesture. A secular mystic, refusing food, infused with a drive which Nazism (she had sensed it) would heat to incandescence, with her insubordination and the rejection it prompted, she strangely resembled the all too human and inhuman Antigone, as revised and corrected by Lacan: neither angel nor demon, but transmitter of truth, transparent to the world by virtue of wasting away, as her friend Georges Bataille underlined.

I confess that I never really subscribed to this ethics of psychoanalysis, whose spokesman Lacan considered himself. Certainly, I regarded as justified the summons not to give way on one's desire, not to stick to the

---

6. I prefer this interpretation to that of Slavoj Žižek, who makes Antigone's 'no' to Creon a female act whose negativity leads her to her own destruction. The tragic is not saying no, but the impossibility of not saying no on pain of dishonour. In other words, Antigone does not enjoy her own destruction. Cf. Slavoj Žižek, *Enjoy Your Symptom! Jacques Lacan in Hollywood and Out*, New York, Routledge, 1992.

alleged virtues of the beautiful soul or emotion displayed to excess, and to make the experience of therapy a way of lucidly facing death, anxiety, oneself. However, with the passage of time, and particularly with the procedure of the 'pass',[7] introduced by Lacan into his school after the events of May 1968, this ethics no longer had anything in common with the tragedy of the 'between-two-deaths', or with the legacy of the Resistance. Alas, it took the form of a commitment that led numerous practitioners from two successive generations to lose interest in subjective suffering: short sessions, silence, inflexible attitude, absence of empathy, frustrations visited on patients, ridiculous interpretations of alleged signifiers, and the use of neologisms instead of clinical discourse.

In short, in the name of the sacrifice of Oedipus' accursed daughter, over thirty years we witnessed the development of interminable therapy during which the analyst, well versed in the religion of 'not giving way on one's desire', ended up making herself the agent of a veritable farce, which radical anti-Freudians have delighted in ridiculing. Even worse, from the height of their arrogance some psychoanalysts began to believe that their doctrine was self-sufficient and exempted them from any political commitment, any social choices. Thus, the 'neutrality' indispensable to the position of the clinician

---

7. A transitional procedure which consists in a future practitioner explaining her desire to become an analyst before an audience of her peers. This procedure was a failure, leading to the dissolution of the EFP. Cf. Élisabeth Roudinesco, *Histoire de la psychanalyse en France*, Paris, Livre de Poche, 2009.

in the transference served the interests of an a-politicism verging on the ridiculous: 'I have nothing to say other than what my practice teaches me; I abstain from taking any positions; I do not publicly respond to the crudest attacks on Freud; I do not get mixed up in anything and I scorn not only my enemies, but my more combative colleagues, who would do better not to express views on fascism, racism, homophobia.' Silence in therapy, silence in the city! Such, alas, was the vulgate shared by a profession for years. And it was met with detestation.

It is true that Lacanians were not the only ones to transform therapy into an interminable, silent, frustrating adventure. For if non-Lacanian Freudians retained the traditional framework of the session of fixed duration, they nonetheless made the mistake of ignoring the fact that psychoanalysis, as a clinical treatment of the subject and the unconscious, and as a theory of reflexion on the self, must be able to respond to all situations and all the demands of subjects in pain. This, moreover, is what Freud encouraged: he spoke and intervened in the course of long sessions and, on occasion, also conducted short treatments while expressing himself on all manner of subjects.

Today, it is advisable to employ a new practice of therapy, a new psychoanalysis that is more open and more attentive to contemporary malaises, misery, the new rights of minorities and the progress of science. Return to Freud, yes; unfaithful re-reading of Lacan, certainly – but far removed from any orthodoxy or nostalgia for a vanished past.

And then let us draw inspiration from the relevance of the interpretation of Antigone with which Lacan made reflection on genocide the precondition for a renaissance of psychoanalysis. This gesture is still valid today: psychoanalysis cannot be anything other than an advance of civilization over barbarism.

Since Lacan substituted Antigone for Oedipus in order to conceive the renewal of psychoanalysis, why not reread his interpretation by showing that Antigone is also the heir to a major transgression – sister of her father and grand-daughter of her mother – which sows disorder in the organization of kinship systems; and that, in this respect, she is the best modern antidote to familialist psychology, which enables supporters of the moral order to oppose new forms of parenthood derived from the disjunction of anatomical order from psychic order, sex from gender, the biological from the social.

And this is not to reckon with the fact that we shall one day have to accept that all the forms of procreation and filiation which underlie new ways of conceiving the family must be controlled by law, from same-sex parenthood, via embryo selection permitting treatment of genetic illnesses, to surrogacy. Antigone would then embody both transgression of the family order and the remedy for that transgression.[8]

---

8. On this point I share Judith Butler's position in *Antigone's Claim: Kinship Between Life and Death*, New York, Columbia University Press, 2002.

KANT WITH DE SADE

Although never a major clinician of sexual perver-
sions – any more than Freud was – Lacan was an
assiduous reader of the oeuvre of de Sade. It was
through Georges Bataille that he became aware of
him, and in a context – the publication of Foucault's
Histoire de la folie – in which de Sade figured as the
hero of an absolute unreason. Lacan had no hesitation in invoking the concentration-camp universe on
numerous occasions, sometimes even going so far as
to identify the lifestyles of western society – its ageing,
pleasures and mass organization – with a totalitarian
nightmare. Returning discontented one day from holidays he had spent in the mountains, he declared that
'winter sports are a kind of concentration camp for
affluent old age, which, as everyone knows, will
become a growing problem in the advance of

civilization, given the increase in the average age over time'.[1]

On the same occasion he also gave free rein to his jealousy of Albert Camus, criticizing him for never having taken into account the issue of the camps in his work and for having 'suppressed' it, like many other 'travelling salesmen' of literature. In doing so, he seemed to ignore the fact that Camus had indeed evoked this issue – metaphorically, obviously – in the novel that earned him the Nobel Prize: *The Plague*. Through the story of the progress of a monstrous epidemic striking the city of Oran, in which rats play a major role, Camus dramatized character types embodying the law, submissiveness, rebellion, passive acceptance of reality, courage, cowardice, and so forth. This theme was not foreign to the one Lacan was fond of; and it is probably here that the underlying reasons for his fury are to be sought.

However, it was in connection with de Sade, not on the occasion of such allusions – somewhat ridiculous, but frequent in his prose – that Lacan picked up the threads of the magisterial analysis he had initiated in his confrontation with Antigone.

As we know, de Sade had proved capable of resisting three political regimes and ended his life in the asylum of Charenton organizing a theatre of madness against the newly established psychiatric order. In it de Sade

---

1. Jacques Lacan, *Le Séminaire. Livre X, L'Angoisse* (1962–63), Paris, Seuil, 1982, p. 173, session of 27 February 1963.

had presented himself as the most virtuous playwright and therapist of his time, by writing plays acted by patients who ended up rejecting the benefits of this experience.

The Sadeian ideal of a subversion of society and an inversion of the highest good into radical evil had been considered in 1947 by Adorno and Horkheimer in *Dialectic of Enlightenment*, which associated the names of Kant and de Sade to make *Juliette*, heroine of the rewards of vice, the dialectical moment of an inversion of reason into its opposite.[2] In the history of western thought, according to the authors, enjoyment of regression was then transformed into a pleasure in destroying civilization that issued into a kind of devastation of culture by industrial capitalism. And from this they deduced that de Sade's inversion of the Law heralded the totalitarian era.[3] In other words, in their view de Sade had put an end to the sacred cycle of carnivalesque orgies. But if he 'desublimated' love and sex, he also revealed what western thought repressed and what Kant imposed an ethics on – the two moves being dialectically linked.

At the time when Lacan likewise seriously reflected on this problematic – 1961 – Hannah Arendt attended Adolf Eichmann's trial in Jerusalem and observed that

---

2. Theodor Adorno and Max Horkheimer, *Dialectic of Enlightenment*, trans. John Cumming, London, Verso, 1986, Excursus II. Horkheimer was the author of this section.

3. In any event, contrary to a simplistic vulgate, they did not claim that de Sade's oeuvre prefigured Nazism or that the Marquis was a kind of SS officer *avant la lettre*.

the person responsible for the extermination of more than five million Jews displayed no apparent sign of pathology. He could be reckoned 'normal', because he had made himself the agent of an inversion of the Law that had made crime the norm. Arendt stressed that, in invoking Kantian philosophy, Eichmann was not prevaricating, because in his view the odious character of the order given counted for nothing compared with the imperative character of the order itself. He had therefore become genocidal without experiencing the slightest guilt and while being fully conscious of the abomination of his acts. He also refused to be judged on an individual basis. However, as Catherine Clément has appropriately stressed, he forgot that for Kant the universal Law always presupposes that man is treated as an end, never as a means.[4]

But the Sadeian ideal of inversion also targeted the status of insanity. If de Sade wanted to cure the patients at Charenton, in *Juliette*, via the character of Vespoli, administrator of the house of correction in Salerno, he had also dreamed of uniting unreason and insanity, knowledge perverted to the point of delirium. He had in fact imagined the principle of an asylum directed by a pervert: ' "The arse of a lunatic – what a delight", said

---

4. Hannah Arendt stresses that he was, above all, very stupid, thus adopting the thesis of stupidity as radical evil and source of the 'banality of evil': see Arendt, *Eichmann in Jerusalem*, London, Penguin, 2006. On stupidity, cf. Élisabeth Roudinesco, *Retour sur la question juive*, Paris, Albin Michel, 2009, p. 204. See also Catherine Clément, 'Freud, la faute, la culpabilité', *Le Magazine littéraire*, no. 367, July/August 1997.

Vespoli! "And me too, I'm mad, twice damned God. I bugger lunatics; I ejaculate in lunatics. I'm crazy for them and they're the only thing on earth I want to screw." [5]

Those who, under the Empire, had sent de Sade to Charenton to silence him knew that he did not belong to the category of lunatics, but was instead the prince of perverts, the emperor of unreason: 'His insanity consisted in perverting', said Antoine Royer-Collard in 1805. 'Society cannot hope to treat him. Thus he must be subjected to the strictest confinement ... He preaches his horrible doctrine to some; he lends his books to others.' [6]

Lacan owned several editions of the Marquis' works at a time when they were not freely on sale. Knowing his taste for libertines, the director of the Cercle du livre précieux suggested that he write a preface to a volume collecting *Justine* and *Philosophy in the Bedroom*. Lacan gave it a now famous title: 'Kant with Sade'. Deemed too hermetic, the text was not accepted by the publisher and Lacan published it in the journal *Critique* in 1963. [7]

---

5. De Sade, *Histoire de Juliette, ou les Prosperités du vice*, in *Oeuvres*, Vol. III, Bibliothèque de la Pléiade, Paris, Gallimard, 1998, p. 1070.

6. I have studied the case of de Sade in *Our Dark Side: A History of Perversion*, trans. David Macey, Cambridge, Polity Press, 2009, Chapter 2, 'Sade Pro and Contra Sade'.

7. In October 1966, with the republication of the *Oeuvres complètes* by the same publisher, the text 'Kant with Sade' was included as a postface after having been revised by Lacan. This 1966 version was then republished in 1980 in the Club du livre secret by Éditions Borderie. The text that appears in the *Écrits*, also published in the fourth quarter of 1966 by Seuil, and corrected by François Wahl, is

I have chosen to return to it once again, because it attests to the way in which Lacan, without naming it as such, was obsessed by the issue of the extermination and its consequences for today's world: what is a crime of man against man as man? What is the *jouissance* of evil? Why has the infernal couple of executioner and victim become so prominent in our ways of living, in literature and in art? How are we to face death in a world that no longer wants heroism?

Lacan had closely followed the work of the Nuremberg Tribunal and, via Jean Delay, had knowledge of the file of Rudolf Hess, about whom he planned to write a case study.

'Kant with Sade' was the logical continuation of the commentary on Antigone. Without citing Adorno or Arendt, Lacan substituted de Sade for Antigone. In his view, both were major figures of disobedience to the law of the city – behaviour which they adopted at the cost of their own destruction. But both also referred to the interminable saga of the two sisters of de Sade's narrative: Justine and Juliette – the one virtuous and condemned to misfortunes, the other vicious and destined for rewards.

Alongside Antigone and de Sade, Lacan summoned Kant and the German Enlightenment. Adopting Foucault's thesis, which counter-posed Pinel, founder

---

different. The order of the different versions is thus as follows: the 1963 text published in *Critique*; that of the *Écrits* in 1966; that of the Cercle du livre précieux, likewise in 1966; the one published in *Écrits* in the 'Points' collection in 1971; and the reprint of the 1980 version by the Club du livre secret.

of moral therapy and the asylum, to de Sade, organizer of a 'nothingness of unreason' and 'sovereign abolition' of oneself, he treated Kant and de Sade equally. Or rather, as the title of his contribution indicates, he thought Kant *with* de Sade: never one without the other. Thus he made the Marquis' work the starting-point of a pervasive rise throughout the nineteenth century of the theme of 'happiness in evil'. He viewed de Sade as the inventor of a new theorization of perversion and his oeuvre as the *'inaugural step* in a subversion whose *turning point* was Kant'.

By dint of this interpretation, evil in the Sadeian sense was presented as an equivalent of the good according to Kant. Both authors formulated the principle of a subject's submission to the Law. However, if we follow Lacan, whereas de Sade conjured up the *Other* in the figure of the tormentor, exhibiting the existence of the object of desire (*little a*), Kant conjured up the same object to contain it, thanks to a theory of the autonomization of the subject by law. In de Sade's discourse, the duty of *jouissance* was foregrounded and desire remained bound to the Law as a voluntaristic instrument of freedom: 'You must take your pleasure.' In Kant's discourse, by contrast, the putting to death of desire was conveyed by the moral Law: 'You must free yourself from pathology.'

Thus, on Lacan's reading of it, Kantian morality was itself derived from a theory of desire in which the object was repressed. This repression was then 'illuminated' by de Sade's discourse. A certain symmetry therefore obtained between de Sade's imperative of *jouissance* and Kant's categorical imperative.

At the moment of the foundation of the EFP in 1964, Lacan claimed that Marxism and Hegelianism were insufficient for thinking the Holocaust. For in this modern tragedy, he said, the highest form of sacrifice to the dark god (assimilated to the big Other) was given free rein. And he went on to cite Spinoza as the only philosopher capable of thinking the eternal meaning of the sacrifice in the *amor intellectualis*.

However, having placed Spinoza in a position of exceptionality, he called for a supersession of philosophy by psychoanalysis, without for all that disowning the content of 'Kant with Sade'. And, notwithstanding the use of the word holocaust (sacrifice), he rejected any theologization of the issue of genocide, be it religious in inspiration or atheist: neither sacrificial debasement of man, nor senseless event abolishing the divine order. Lacan therefore universalized Auschwitz, making it the tragedy of the century proper to humanity as a whole.

Lacan claimed to be convinced that post-Freudian clinical treatment of neurosis and psychosis, whether Kantian or, on the contrary, derived from ego psychology, did not make it possible to think the consequences of this event in the history of humanity. In other words, an understanding of the reality and posterity of such an atrocity was facilitated neither by a return to the archaic body of the mother, nor by transcendence of the death instinct in favour of an autonomized ego, nor by an appeal to the benefits of hedonism. Basically, having substituted Antigone for Oedipus, Lacan was not far from thinking that perverse desire was now the model, heroized or hated, of the new social relations peculiar to the individualism of the modern democratic world: destroying the other, rather than accepting conflict.

Freud, classical clinician of hysteria and conflict within the bourgeois family, had glimpsed this problematic at the end his life, through his analysis of 'civilization and its discontents'. But in order to grasp its metamorphoses, it was further necessary, so Lacan argued, to consider the issue of the perverse subject – and hence perverse desire – and not confine oneself to the framework of an 'Oedipal' psychology. And to support this position, he constantly revisited the great texts of western literature, from Sophocles to Joyce, via Shakespeare, de Sade, Claudel, Duras and Genet. More of a 'speculator' than Freud, Lacan nevertheless remained a conscientious reader throughout his life, drawing on the literary tradition for his sources.

It is therefore no cause for surprise if 'Kant with Sade' has often been commented on, in contradictory fashion, from one end of the planet to the other, by all thinkers of postmodernity. Some identified Lacan as a pervert of civilization, fascinated by executioners and sadism, while others regarded him as the propagator of a new familialist order based on the rehabilitation of paternal authority, or, on the contrary, as the artisan of a transgender or transsexual revolution leading woman to be of both sexes. Finally, others made 'Kant with Sade' into the tool of a critique of Sadeian liberal society assimilated to a new totalitarianism: Kant embodying Stalin and de Sade the trans-Atlantic libidinal subject.[8]

Having reached this point of the problematic, I would like to recall that Lacan believed transgression to be as necessary to civilization as the symbolic order which made it possible to remedy it. And this is the hypothesis I myself endorsed when I undertook to study the history of perversion. Such is the humanist lesson of 'Kant with Sade', corollary of the substitution of Antigone for Oedipus. But this text is also like Lacan himself, at once transgressive and attached to the idea that the Law alone is capable of setting limits to the desire to enjoy things, objects, humans and non-humans.

Speaking one day of his favourite animal, Lacan flung this sentence at his dumbfounded audience: 'I have a female dog that I have called Justine, in homage to de Sade, without (take my word for it) inflicting on her any one-sided abuse.'[9]

---

8. Such is the thesis, in particular, of Slavoj Žižek.
9. Jacques Lacan, *Le Séminaire. Livre IX, L'Identification* (1961–62), unpublished text, session of 29 September 1961.

DEATH

In autumn 1978 Lacan had a car accident while driving his white Mercedes. He emerged unscathed. But to those around him he gave the impression of being diminished. His tiredness grew worse and his silences lasted longer. For its twenty-sixth year his seminar was due to focus on 'Topology and Time'. During the first session on 21 November, Lacan lost the power of speech in front of his audience, which remained as silent as him. Everyone could see the old man beset by immense weariness and deprived of the voice which, for a quarter-century, had held generations of intellectuals and psychoanalysts spellbound.

While he was drawing his knots and plaits on the blackboard, Lacan became confused, turned towards the audience, spoke of his mistake, and then left the room. 'No matter,' people were heard to murmur, 'we still love you.'

In September 1979 a journalist wrote a crazy article in which he compared Lacan to the Ayatollah Khomeini:[1] 'You don't fire on an ambulance', he said in conclusion. The next day, hundreds of letters, sent from every corner of France, arrived at the newspaper, written not only by intimates and intellectuals, but also by anonymous people who obviously had not read his work: psychiatric nurses, specialist teachers, social workers, educational psychologists, patients. The journalist had forgotten how popular Lacan was – not the Lacan of knots, Antigone or 'Kant with Sade', but the psychiatrist, the doctor of the insane, the one who for half a century, together with some fellow-travellers, supporters of the common good and public service, had embodied the ideals of an institutional psychotherapy and a humanist psychiatry, today in disarray. Following the publication of my *History of Psychoanalysis*, I frequently realized how alive the name of Lacan remained in the collective memory of all these practitioners of psychic suffering. And it still is today.

From December 1979 onwards, some began to say that Lacan was applying himself to remaining silent so as to hear better; that he was still fully lucid and his hearing perfect. People sought to ignore the terrible suffering that ravaged him and which was expressed by face spasms. No more voice, no more words. I had occasion to speak to him then. His face was already turned to the world of an infinite silence and his expression

1. *Le Monde*, 21 September 1979.

remained elusive, as if attracted by that immemorial elsewhere. Lacan was afraid of ageing, of dying, of no longer seducing. In him were combined Don Juan and the statue of the Commendatore.

On 9 September 1981, Lacan died under a false name in the Hartmann Clinic of a cancer of the colon that he never wanted treated. He was buried privately, and without ceremony, in the Guitrancourt cemetery. He had thought of ending his days in Italy, in Rome or Venice, and one day, although a materialist, out of bravado had even dreamed of a grand Catholic funeral.

Libération, the most Lacanian of the French newspapers, paid him a beautiful tribute by mixing background articles with slogans that resembled him: '*Tout fou Lacan*', '*Lacan fait le mort comme tout le monde*', '*Lacan n'est plus*', '*Lacan même*'.[2] That Lacan – the Lacan of an avalanche of words, things, lists, collections, places, discrepant objects, of the inversion of meanings, the gap, insatiable *jouissance*, the origin of the world, of hatred provoked and reciprocated, of such bravado – I too remember him, thirty years after his death.

Lacan in spite of everything.

---

2. *Libération*, 11 September 1981.

INDEX

A NOTE ON THE TYPE

This book is set in Sabon, a narrow Garamond-style book face designed in 1968 by the German typographer Jan Tschichold. Tschichold had been a leading voice of sans-serif modernist typography, particularly after the publication of his *Die neue Typographie* in 1928. As a result, the Nazis charged him with "cultural Bolshevism" and forced him to flee Germany for Switzerland.

Tschichold soon renounced modernism—comparing its stringent tenets to the "teachings of National Socialism and fascism"—and extolled the qualities of classical typography, exemplified in his design for Sabon, which he based on the Romain S. Augustin de Garamond in the 1592 Egenolff-Berner specimen sheet.

Sabon is named after the sixteenth-century French type-founder Jacques Sabon, a pupil of Claude Garamond and proprietor of the Egenolff foundry.